Praise for Frank Deford and *I'd Know That Voice Anywhere*

"Frank Deford is the best sportswriter I've ever read . . . If there's a Mount Rushmore of sportswriting, Deford is up there, purple ties and all." —Tony Kornheiser

"One of the greatest writers of our time." —Billie Jean King

"Frank Deford . . . writes with more graceful good humor than any man I know." —Richard Ben Cramer

"Deford . . . is the handsome, swashbuckling man of sports journalism. For fifty years, he has been issuing perhaps the greatest writing the realm has known." —*Chicago Sun-Times*

"Deford's cred is incredible, his accolades deserved . . . [He] has long been the genuine article." —*Los Angeles Times*

"Deford is the Holy Grail. He's simply one of the greatest sportswriters of all time." —Peter King, SI.com

"Thank heaven for Frank Deford." —*San Antonio Express-News*

"Wonderful . . . Deford's new book underscores his brilliance as a writer . . . Deford fans are well-advised to check [it] out." —*Poynter*

"A sparkling sampler of commentaries from celebrated sports journalist Frank Deford . . . This prime selection of Deford's most insightful NPR pieces offers a kaleidoscope of sports highs and lows . . . *I'd Know That Voice Anywhere* is an eclectic joy to read, highly recommended." —*Midwest Book Review*

"Deford . . . has a wickedly droll sense of humor, which, when coupled with his encyclopedic knowledge of sports, results in commentaries that are incisive, amusing, touching, or incendiary in various combinations . . . A rich collection for anyone interested in the sporting life." —*Booklist*

"An eclectic collection . . . [Deford] could make a shopping list interesting to read." —*Buffalo News*

Also by Frank Deford

FICTION
Cut 'n' Run
The Owner
Everybody's All-American
The Spy in the Deuce Court
Casey on the Loose
Love and Infamy
The Other Adonis
An American Summer
The Entitled
Bliss, Remembered

NONFICTION
Five Strides on the Banked Track
There She Is
Big Bill Tilden
Alex: The Life of a Child
The World's Tallest Midget
The Best of Frank Deford
The Old Ball Game
Over Time

I'd Know That Voice Anywhere

My Favorite **NPR** *Commentaries*

Frank Deford

Grove Press
New York

Copyright © 2016 by Frank Deford

"Words to Play By," "Where Have We Gone?" (originally published as "A Man for His Times"), "Chicago" (originally published as "Our American City"), "Play a Fore" (originally published as "Golf v. Tennis"), "Too Much to Care" (originally published as "Worth"), "The Forgotten (Well, Briefly)" (originally published as "Just Like Switzerland"), "Gone Fishin'," "Gimme That Old-Time Momentum" (originally published as "Momentum Has Momentum"), and "Speaking of Sports" (originally published as "Sports Centered") first appeared in *The Best of Frank Deford* (Triumph Books, 2000).

All rights reserved. No part of this book may be reproduced in any form or by any electronic or mechanical means, including information storage and retrieval systems, without permission in writing from the publisher, except by a reviewer, who may quote brief passages in a review. Scanning, uploading, and electronic distribution of this book or the facilitation of such without the permission of the publisher is prohibited. Please purchase only authorized electronic editions, and do not participate in or encourage electronic piracy of copyrighted materials. Your support of the author's rights is appreciated. Any member of educational institutions wishing to photocopy part or all of the work for classroom use, or anthology, should send inquiries to Grove Atlantic, 154 West 14th Street, New York, NY 10011 or permissions@groveatlantic.com.

Published simultaneously in Canada
Printed in the United States of America

First Grove Atlantic hardcover edition: May 2016
First Grove Atlantic paperback edition: May 2017

ISBN 978-0-8021-2672-6
eISBN 978-0-8021-9035-2

Grove Press
an imprint of Grove Atlantic
154 West 14th Street
New York, NY 10011

Distributed by Publishers Group West

groveatlantic.com

17 18 19 20   10 9 8 7 6 5 4 3 2 1

For Scarlet and Sean Crawford

Contents

Nine Innings, Four Periods,
and an Overtime

Foreword   xiii

ONE

Mass and Class, Together	3
Words to Play By	5
Our Indecent Joys	8
Sisters, 1 and 1-A	10
By the Seat of Their Pants	12
The Groundhog Games	15
Back in the Day	18

TWO

Sports Are in the Union, Too?	23
Spittin' Image	25
The Other Winnie-the-Pooh	28
Little Big Man	31
Stoodint Athaleets	33
The Real Bad Guys	35
The Volunteer State	38

THREE

The Pursuit of Sports   45
Baseball's Sad Lexicon   47
To an Athlete Leaving Young   50
The All-Purpose Sports Movie   52
The Other Sports Violence   55
Another Way to Win   58
Par for the Course   60

FOUR

The Super Bard   65
Worse Even Than Us?   69
Where Have We Gone?   71
Me and Paul   74
Bad Bubbly   76
We're Number 33!   78
Trading Up   80

FIVE

Football Are Us   85
The Victim   87
Euro Exceptionalism   89
I Can Work Longer Than You   91
The Snakes in the Garden of Sports   93
Chicago   95
Put an End to It   98

SIX

Give and Go   103
Pretty Good   105

Mister Misses   107
His Refuge   109
You're It Is Out   111
The Last in the Line   113
Hailing Proudly Too Often   115

SEVEN

Kept Men   121
Seashells and Balloons   123
Keeping the Elephants Away   126
Real vs. Reality   129
That Sunday of Ours   132
Play a Fore   135
Home Alone   137

EIGHT

Match Play   143
Up to Speed   146
Did He Say That?   148
Da Boys Will Be Boys   150
Time to Go   152
A Good Aim   154
Deliverance   156

NINE

Who Needs War?   161
Headmaster   163
Girl Watching   165
Too Much to Care   167
Namesake   170

The Patriots Act   172
The Forgotten (Well, Briefly)   175

TEN

All Guys All the Time   179
Loyal (Sports) Alumni   181
The Old Butterfly   183
Sound Off   185
Past-ism   187
Let's Give 'Em a Hand   189
Southern Comfort   191

ELEVEN

Artful   195
Gone Fishin'   197
Nouveau Heart and Mind   200
Little Big Man   202
Life in the Time of Drugs   204
GMs and ADs   206
End of a Love Affair   208

TWELVE

Presidential Exploitation   213
Wistful Day   215
Fat Chance   218
Game Changer   221
There's No "I" in U.S.A.   223
Gimme That Old-Time Momentum   225
Mulligans   227

THIRTEEN

The Other State U's 231

The Fenway Park Address 234

Getting to Know You 236

Patriot Games 238

August Song 241

The Rev. Mr. Coach 243

Used to Be 246

FOURTEEN

Blessed Are the Pure 251

Speaking of Sports 253

Life Among the Idle Fans 256

Juiced 259

Don't Tie One On 262

Paying Through the Noseguard 264

Sweetness and Light 267

Foreword

Being a writer, I never paid much attention to my voice. Since, when it came to interviewing, I was a primitive pen-and-notebook reporter, I rarely even heard myself speak on a tape recorder. Inasmuch as I can't carry a tune, I certainly never sang. Much of my life was conducted before answering machines came along. I just figured I got by speaking to other people with a nice, everyday speaking voice.

Then, in the autumn of 1979, through impossibly seren-dipitous circumstances, National Public Radio approached me about doing a weekly sports commentary, and suddenly I had to direct that run-of-the-mill voice of mine into a microphone. But then, to my utter delight (shock and awe?), I soon found myself being complimented, advised that I possessed a distinct "radio voice." *Where did you get that?* people asked me, as if you could pick it out at an appliance store.

I had grown up in Baltimore, where many of the natives speak in abrasive, nasal tones. Somehow I had avoided picking up that patois. My mother came from Richmond, and so it is possible that, via the miracle of genes, a bit of her southern lilt found its way to my vocal cords. Then, postadolescence, as I moved from Baltimore to the more cosmopolitan precincts of Princeton and Manhattan, my tongue may have picked up some gravitas to balance the inherited Dixie syrup. My wife taught me how not to butcher French words, to sound more *savoir-faire*. And, if I do say so myself, I think I own a naturally superior chuckle. (An accomplished chuckle is a rare radio gift, just right for leavening and far more valuable on the air than is a hearty laugh.) I've finally decided that I must possess what may be best described as the domestic version of a mid-Atlantic accent.

Anyway, I was advised that something set my bloviation machinery apart . . . at least for the perceptive folk listening to NPR. I've even had strangers who do not know what I look like, but who have merely heard me talking to friends in, say, some relatively subdued saloon, approach me and inquire if I wasn't Frank Deford. That voice. *I would know it anywhere.*

Even the high and mighty have said the same. When I introduced myself to Hillary Clinton in the receiving line at a black-tie White House event, the first lady's response was, "Oh, I'd know you anywhere, Frank. That voice wakes me up every Wednesday morning."

So, quite to my surprise, I possessed the physical goods for approved radio transmission, just as the writer in me came to love my three dramatic minutes a week when I could *voice* my own wise words in front of the NPR microphone. Please understand, too, that, in the vernacular, I mean that precisely, for "voice" is the operative verb of choice at NPR for verbalizing. Usually, in the world at large, the verb *voice* is used only with the predicate "his objections," but at NPR, it is how we describe what we do, live or recorded. Thus, listeners hear me voice three minutes on Wednesday mornings that I have previously voiced on a fancy recording device, i.e., what used to be called "tape."

In any event, as I became a regular on the national airwaves, I recalled what Howard Cosell (now *there* was a distinct voice) had told me once, that as awesome as the written word could be, and even though we know that one lousy picture is worth a thousand of those words, and on top of that television is the most powerful medium ever invented, never mind, Mr. Cosell informed me: a proper voice emanating from a radio may carry the most weight of all. That is because, he declared, a radio voice is simple and direct and comes to the listener without visual distractions.

The ultimate: Paul Harvey: "Gooddd . . . day!"

The penultimate: H. Cosell: "This reporter has learned . . ."

Given that this is a printed page, a whole book in the aggregate, it may seem odd that I would start off immodestly analyzing, even rhapsodizing about, my delivery, but I am intrigued at this proposition that what I have spoken/voiced for the ear is here seeking to catch the approval of the eye. It's unusual, maybe even risky, to attempt such a particular trans-communication. Most books that are an accumulation of shorter pieces are filled with the assembled likes of essays or short stories or columns— that is, other works that were likewise originally printed. Sermons, I think, are the rare audio disquisition that sometimes make a successful leap from the utterance to the page. But then, of course, sermons have faith going for them.

Nowadays, there's probably more crossover headed in the other direction, written words being given a second exposure by a vocal professional—books on tape. Myself, once I left my mother's lap, I've never heard a book read to me that I found as enjoyable as when I read it myself. However, I would say that in both cases where language is taken into an alternative realm the new medium does possess one advantage over the original rendering.

In the one instance, the actor reading a book for you on a CD can dramatize the written word, give it the pizzazz that a writer just can't gin up by himself no matter how talented he might be. (That's why we have actors in the first place, isn't it?) And I'm not just talking about action and mystery and scary stuff. To me, the Gettysburg Address always comes across much better when read aloud than it does merely being absorbed in print. I wonder how emotional Lincoln—who was apparently distinguished by a curiously high voice—was in reading it.

Ah, but the other way around: the great advantage anyone reading something always has over being a mere captive listener is that the reader can conveniently pause and reread what she is tackling, make sure she understands clearly what is being foisted on her by the writer. I know that on NPR I can sneak by with a clever fillip, a nice turn of phrase—not unlike Father Abraham ripping off *dedicate, consecrate, hallow*, bing, bing, bing—whereas if I was writing the same material out I would be much more careful in illuminating my point in detail (as I'm doing now). Not to be facetious, but just to stick with the same example, if Lincoln had not *delivered* the Gettysburg Address, but written it as an op-ed, how much longer would he have gone on? Lots, I'll bet.

So, yes, I do worry that when you read these erstwhile voiced words of mine they won't strike as clear a note as they did had you heard them tripping glibly off my tongue one fine mornin' while you were combing your hair or waiting for the red light to change.

Be assured, though, that I played fair. I only tinkered with a handful of words in a few of the pieces, changing the language just a bit where I felt that the translation from the ear to the eye just didn't hold up. So, I promise: the NPR commentaries I've chosen to print here are, as Ivory Soap used to assure us, ninety-nine and forty-four one-hundredths percent pure . . . NPR.

Actually, I know how fortunate I am to be able to address the NPR audience. Sports reporting, in whatever medium it may be found, is invariably isolated in an all-sports niche: the sports section, sports radio, ESPN, *Sports Illustrated*. If you are not interested in sports, it's quite easy to avoid ever having to encounter any sports analysis. But the NPR audience is broad and the *broad*cast purposely includes a mélange of subjects, so that I am able to reach so many people who otherwise don't care all that much about sports. To be sure, some listeners who hear my allotted three minutes can't abide to suffer even that small snippet of jock chat. I understand that. After all, H. L. Mencken, the notorious sage from my hometown, once said: "I hate sports as rabidly as a person who likes sports hates common sense." So, yes, I know there are those as rabid still, and some are tuned to NPR. But many others who are ignorant of sports, but who are of the open-minded ilk, have told me that they quite like me briefly taking them down a rabbit hole they otherwise wouldn't ever tumble into. (Of course, as a friend advised me, this does mean that a substantial number of my most devoted fans really don't know what the hell I'm talking about.)

But, honestly, I do relish the fact that I'm reaching a cohort of Americans who aren't sports fans. Most important, this allows me to talk about sports in broad terms, trying to connect them to our culture and paint sport large, rather than having to indulge in the minutiae, the x's and o's, the skinny. Thank God, I don't have to *predict!*

I would say that the most difficult part of the job is coming up with enough original subject matter. Not only is sports a fairly limited bailiwick, but the commentator/columnist in any area of the news invariably struggles with the constant demand to produce new lamps for old. I believe it was Red Smith who described the deadline agony of writing a regular column as being only a matter of sitting there before the typewriter "until little drops of blood appear on your forehead." I know the feeling. Sometimes, in abject desperation, I even fervently hope someone dies. Not anyone in particular, you understand—but just some fond, random old hero whom I can eulogize.

I do believe, too, that, to the best of my ability, I should vary the tone and content of my pieces from week to week. If

I'm up on a soapbox one week, say, eviscerating the NCAA (my critics invariably say I'm "ranting" on these occasions), then I'll at least try to come up with something lighter, rant-free, next time around.

I've sought to arrange this printed collection in the same way, so that the order is intentionally eclectic. The last thing I wanted to do was to sequester all the football commentaries in one pigskin premium section, the lighter fare in other friendly confines—or make it so that the reader had to trace through it all chronologically, like an athlete summarizing his seasons, the one after another. I've arranged the pieces in chunks of seven, just because that seemed like a nice, odd number otherwise given over to deadly sins, dwarfs, and wonders of the world; it just seemed to be the right pants size. So, as much as possible, the order is varied, like sport itself—the serious, the foolish, the noble, the idiosyncratic; this game, that athlete. In this sense, I fear it lacks that old sports reliable—momentum. Rather, I hope I've managed to be more like a canny old veteran pitcher, changing speeds, mixing up his stuff.

Well, canny or not, I certainly qualify as a veteran now. I started voicing these commentaries in April of 1980, when it occurred to someone at NPR that the new show, *Morning Edition*, should offer at least a soupçon of sports. I was then a writer at *Sports Illustrated*, and, for whatever reason, my work there suggested that I might be the sort of fellow who could cobble together radio commentaries, as well. Then, when I was approached, I thought it sounded like a fun thing to try for, oh, six or eight months. It wasn't the money.

The late Red Barber, by turns delightful and thoughtful, was my colleague, an alternative sports voice back in those halcyon days. While I delivered the set pieces, Red was wonderfully anecdotal, idly chatting with Bob Edwards, then the show's engaging host. In sports argot, Red was a wide receiver, running original routes, while I was coming out of the back-field, looking for holes to open up.

I did have to give up the NPR microphone for a couple of years, 1989–91, while I edited a daily sports paper, *The National*, but, alas, that noble journal folded. However as we are wont to say in the business, then I inked a new pact and returned to the NPR fold, hoping not to have lost a step. Since then, in that intervening twenty-four years, while I've had a pleth-ora of NPR producers, almost all of the commentaries were done with just four wonderful engineers—Manoli Wetherell in New York, Geri Diorio and Julie Freddino in Connecticut, and Randy Perry in Key West. All together, since 1980, I've voiced more than 1,600 commentaries and have, assuredly, never once repeated myself nor contradicted myself. Nor repeated myself. Well, to the delight of millions, I've stopped picking on soccer. Those people will just never learn.

I cannot leave off without thanking NPR for giving me the chance to talk about sports—even to rant some—all these years. Sports is, on the one level, mere amusement, but it is found in every culture, and while it's not an absolute necessity for us, as eating and drinking and procreation are—sports is a card-carrying part of the human condition, in the same league with religion and drama and art and music. You can ignore sports, just as you might choose not to care about other of those optional devotions, but sports does have a hefty place in our world, and I'm pleased to have been its troubadour on NPR. To voice sports may well be the next best thing to being out on the field itself, playing. And there's no risk of concussions.

— Frank Deford

ONE

Mass and Class, Together

2007

Perhaps you heard recently when Al Gore observed that the country was too celebrity obsessed. This, he said, was too distracting to hoi polloi—or the *Boobus Americanus*, if you incline more toward Mencken's own Latin assessment of our citizenry—from caring about issues that really matter.

Shortly thereafter, though, Jack Shafer, a media columnist for *Slate*, the online magazine, suggested that the former vice president had missed the greater target.

"If (Gore) possessed any real courage," Shafer wrote, "he'd attack sports coverage"—which, the columnist estimated, must eat up 20 percent of every newspaper's editorial budget. Fair criticism? Are sports fans really lotus eaters? Well, to be sure, there are an awful lot of featherbrained fans who could rattle off the entire roster of the Kansas City Royals before they could name their own congressman.

But somehow I doubt that these folks would suddenly become as acutely involved as informed citizens if, tomorrow, all sports coverage instantly ceased. Probably, in fact, their new devotion would be to something more base, like pornography.

On the other hand, while a lot of intelligent folks do think sports are serious business, I doubt that anybody who even conscientiously follows the high jinks of Lindsay Lohan, Paris Hilton, et al. ever believes that that stuff really matters. It's just a benign retreat from reality.

Actually, although God knows this irony surely didn't occur to Mr. Gore, he was really, unintentionally, singling out women. Yes, it is they, far more than men, who tune in the celebrity programs and buy the gossip magazines. No, please, neither am I dumb enough to castigate women en masse, but I do think that a proportionate devotion to sports—a population which numbers more men, by far—is a healthier escape than the predilection for dunking into the world of boldface.

But remember this, perhaps above all, about sports. In our culture, sports is now the only entertainment where popularity and excellence thrive in tandem. The best movies, the best plays, the best books, the best art, the best music are never nowadays what attracts the most attention. As a matter of fact, popular culture is too often dominated by junk, while true brilliance goes unappreciated.

But sport is different. Those who care about sports are connoisseurs. The best and most artistic and most graceful of the genre is what attracts the most devotion. Paying attention to excellence is so rare in this tacky universe. Sports is the only discipline—on the whole earth, so far as I know—where mass and class are still conjoined.

That doesn't absolve the many abuses in sport. It doesn't excuse the fans who impart too much of their lives to a mere diversion. It does, though, distinguish sport and elevate it above our other popular entertainments.

Words to Play By

1983

Many baseball terms have moved into our everyday vernacular. Every Broadway producer wants to hit a home run. A foul ball is the rascal your daughter is in love with. A good salesman takes a lot of orders by throwing a change of pace. And everybody is now on guard in this world when they hear they're gonna have to play some hardball.

But overlooked, I think—and much more interesting—is how baseball has taken words from the general lexicon and applied them altogether differently to the game.

For example: *deep* and/or *shallow*. Outfielders are deep when they play back, farther from the plate, or shallow when they're closer. So far as I know, this is the only place in our usage where deep and shallow are employed in a lateral sense. Everywhere else, deep or shallow refers to the vertical—as, for example, when a team has a deep pitching staff.

If a batter hits a long ball, he gives it a *ride*. I wonder how that developed? Everywhere else, if you provide a ride, you take something along with you. If baseball patois was like the rest of language, you should *send* a long ball on a trip, rather than give it a ride. In this regard, don't forget that a home run became a "round-trip," but a double never is called a one-way trip.

But then, there is no logic to baseball argot.

Why is a slow pitch an *off*-speed pitch? A slow thorough-bred is not an off-speed runner. Rather, he is a bum, a stiff, or a muskrat. Off invariably has a definitive quality to it. The light is off or it is on. Turn it down or turn it up to provide gradations, but on is on and off is off. You are on the bus or you are off. But only in baseball is off (or on) used in a qualitative sense. He took a little off that pitch. He put something on it.

One of my favorite baseball expressions is *range*—as a verb. A musician has great range. So does a company's product line. So, for that matter, does an outstanding jump shooter in basketball. But only shortstops regularly range deep into the hole. Range, as a baseball verb, is employed more than all the other ranges put together. Nobody ever said, for example, that Bill Clinton ranged more to the center. Why is that?

By far my favorite baseball verb is *shade*. Damn, that's beautiful. Wake me up in the middle of the night and tell me the outfield is shaded to the right, and I can picture exactly what you mean. In fact, is it possible that a lot of this descriptive baseball vocabulary developed on the radio for fans who could not see the game? Or does it date back to antiquity? I can see Spalding or Hanlon or some other nineteenth-century manager in my mind's eye now, coming out of the dugout and screaming to the outfielders to shade to the right.

I'm pretty sure a *breaking* pitch has always been around. Why? If I asked you to describe a curve in the road you would never say it breaks. Possibly breaking pitch comes from the ocean, where a curling wave breaks. And yet, we never say that a curveball explodes, which is, of course, what so often happens when something breaks. Only a fastball explodes, even though a fastball doesn't break.

A batter who hits a ball down the line—that is, a right-handed batter, who slugs the pitch to left field—is said to *pull* the ball. Why? When you pull something in the rest of the world, you bring it to you. Only in baseball do you step into something, swing away, and then have that result identified as a pull.

I also like it when a batter punches the ball the other way (which is a very accurate usage) and it is referred to as *fighting the pitch off*. The reason this fascinates me so is that fighting off is otherwise almost exclusively used in amorous terms. The heroine fights off the cad's advances.

To me, though, perhaps the most intriguing baseball term of all is *take*, as in *he takes the pitch*. Otherwise, take is a very aggressive word. Take a dollar. Take a chance. Take it or leave it. Take a hike. To take a pitch should mean to rip into it and give it a ride . . . excuse me, take it on a trip.

But in baseball, take means not to take.

Take that.

Our Indecent Joys

2013

This may sound far-fetched, but football reminds me of Venice. Both are so tremendously popular, but it's the very things that made them so which could sow the seeds of their ruin. Venice, of course, is so special because of its unique island geography, which, as the world's ecosystems change, is precisely what now puts it at risk. And, as it is the violent nature of football that makes *it* so attractive, the understanding of how that brutality can damage those who play the game is what may threaten it . . . even as now the sport climbs to ever new heights of popularity.

Boxing, another latently cruel sport, has lost most of its standing, so it is often cited as the example of how football too must eventually be doomed in our more refined, civilized society. However, the comparisons between boxing and football don't fly because there is a huge difference between individual and team sports.

Football teams *represent* cities and colleges and schools. The people have built great stadiums, and the game is culturally intertwined with our calendar. We don't go back to college for the college. We go back for a football game, and, yes, we even call that "homecoming." It would take some unimagined cataclysmic event to take football from us. Concussions for young men are the price of our love for football, as broken hearts are what we pay for young love.

Indeed, part of boxing's decline may well be because football has exceeded its display for bloodlust. When George Bellows was painting those graphically gruesome boxing paintings a century ago, he noted that the "atmosphere" around the ring was "more immoral" than the brutality within it. The thrill of *watching* football is not that players perform with such incredible precision, but that they do so even as they dance in the shadow of collision. Enthusiasm for sport can be a convenient cover to excuse the worst in us.

Of course, the difference between the Venice of Italy and the football here is that *everybody* loves Venice, but only Americans care about our gridiron. Football is, and always has been, a sport on the edge of that immorality that Bellows saw when he painted men cheering pain. But then, football is also, and always has been, the presumed proof of American manliness— the sport that was the beau ideal of what was called "muscular Christianity."

Way back in 1896, after the president of Harvard University wanted to ban a sport he called "more brutal than cockfighting or bull-fighting," Henry Cabot Lodge, a senator from Massachusetts, responded by declaring that "the injuries incurred on the playing field are the price which the English-speaking race has paid for being world conquerors."

Have no fear. Football is still our own indecent joy. The fighter jets will long fly over the Super Bowl.

Sisters, 1 and 1-A

2002

I've been very amused lately whenever some new accomplishment of the Williams sisters, Venus and Serena, is mentioned in this fashion: "The first sisters ever to play in the finals of a major tournament," or "The first sisters ever to rank one-two in the world," as if all sorts of other sisters through the years have made the semifinals or been ranked three and four. Let's get this in perspective: what Venus and Serena have achieved, two sisters being the very best in the world at one thing, is not only unique to tennis, not only unique to all major sports, but as far as I know, to all human endeavors. The only brothers I can think of who stood one-two in their field were Wilbur and Orville Wright, and they invented their field.

Well, in tennis, there were the Doherty brothers, Reggie and Laurie, who dominated Wimbledon a century ago, but they were sequential champions. And, anyway, tennis wasn't a much bigger deal than a steak and kidney pie then. Dizzy and Daffy Dean won all four games for the Cardinals in the 1934 World Series, but "me and Paul," so-called by Diz, "weren't the best pitchers overall by any measure."

With Venus and Serena, though, it's as if Mozart and Beethoven were brothers. And, let's get it straight: the Williamses simply are, suddenly, tennis today. They're it, the whole sport. Women's tennis used to be this wonderful championship smorgasbord, but Lindsay Davenport is injured. Martina Hingis is recovering from an operation, happily trailing her boyfriend, Sergio Garcia, about the links. Arantxa Sánchez-Vicario and Monica Seles have grown long in the tooth. And Jennifer Capriati, last year's sweetheart, has morphed into an ungracious churl. All who's left to contend with Venus and Serena are two Belgians and a collection of Eastern Europeans whose names all end in "ova," except, unfortunately, none of them anymore are named Anna Kournik-ova.

No, it's just Venus and Serena now, better, stronger, and even more becoming. Speaking some French in their joint victory and defeat speeches after Serena beat Venus in the Roland Garros final earlier this month was just so attractive, especially at a time when Europeans find Americans so self-centered and superpowerously insensitive to others. So the Williams ladies not only won the French; they won over the French. And if there's a sure bet in sports today, it's that they will get through to the Wimbledon final, rat-a-tat-tatting their power game on the grass.

Unfortunately, that's the problem. Venus and Serena have no passion for playing one another. And tennis, like boxing, thrives on contrast. Somebody once said that a tie is like kissing your sister. And, well, now we know that playing your sister is also like kissing your sister. But then, Venus and Serena can't be blamed if they're simply too good and the finals now are just a sweet embrace of sisterhood.

By the Seat of Their Pants

2001

The tragic death of Dale Earnhardt, particularly coming as it did just as NASCAR had moved into big-time network television, has prompted a great deal more discussion about the justification of automobile racing in our civilized American society. Especially in the North, most especially among old-line sports fans, there's a visceral deep-seated antipathy toward NASCAR.

Just so, as we say, you know where I'm coming from, let me tell you. Automobile racing leaves me cold. Don't take it personally. It's only a matter of taste. I also don't like Picasso, Scotch whiskey, Thanksgiving, or *Forrest Gump*. There are four things that compete on racetracks. I enjoy watching horses and people race, and I don't enjoy watching dogs and cars race.

I also have no affinity for most NASCAR fans. I do not wish to bond with them, and I certainly do not wish to drink beer with them. But having said that, let me also state directly that I do not think for a moment that race fans are bloodthirsty ghouls who go out to the tracks to picnic and to see accidents.

The manifold despair displayed for Mr. Earnhardt's death should dispel that canard all by itself for all time. No, NASCAR

fans love their drivers. They don't want them dead or maimed.
As a matter of fact, I believe that's why car racing is so much
more popular than horses, people, and dogs racing, because
the same drivers compete Sunday after Sunday. And since we
all drive cars, car race fans identify with their heroes, more so,
I think, than do fans of other sports.

The attraction is not seeing an accident. Rather, the attraction is watching drivers *risk* an accident time and time again.
We don't go to the circus to see the lion eat the lion tamer; we
go to marvel at how close the lion tamer came to being eaten.

Critics also like to argue that race car drivers are not real
bona fide athletes. Of course, they are. You can be an athlete
sitting down. Dale Earnhardt was as much, if not more, of an
athlete as is any baseball designated hitter, any PGA golfer, or
any three-hundred-pound lineman stuffing the run.

There's no question in my mind that much of the distaste
for NASCAR has nothing to do with the sport, but is derived
from history and geography. If only General Pickett had had
The Intimidator in car number three leading his charge across
the Gettysburg dale, things would have been very different.

NASCAR, you see, reminds us that the South has risen
again. But it also amuses me that the cries for the abolition of
automobile racing, the captious claim of its barbarism, invariably come from people up North who love boxing and find that
sport manly. Certainly both boxing and automobile racing are
dangerous, but the difference is that boxing is the one where
the intent is to hurt your opponent.

Safety issues in automobile racing? Boxing is anti-safety.
But automobile racing is terribly perilous and before long, as
sure as there will be another chorus of "Dixie" raised from the
infield, some other driver will follow poor Earnhardt to his
grave.

But nobody makes these men climb into their driver seats and none of them are trying to hurt one another. Automobile racing does not insult our morality the way that boxing, the favorite sporting amusement of many intellectuals, does. No, although NASCAR may be too loud and tacky, too fast and garish for many of us, it is a perfectly honorable slice of American life and death.

The Groundhog Games

2012

Why do we like the Olympics?

Or: if somebody hadn't thought to start them up again one hundred and sixteen years ago, would ESPN have invented them to fill in summer programming?

I'm not being cranky. It's just that most of the most popular Olympic sports are really the groundhog games. Swimming, gymnastics, and track and field come out every four years, see their shadow, and go right back underground where nobody pays any attention to them for another four years. Can you even name a gymnast? Okay, track and swimming—maybe you've heard about Usain Bolt and certainly you know Michael Phelps, but that's slim pickin's for two weeks in what's supposed to be a celebrity-driven world.

The Olympics are like an independent movie with foreign actors you've never heard of.

Especially since air travel came along, most sports have their own world championships. The world's athletes don't have to all come together in a smorgasbord every four years anymore. The soccer people are smart. They don't want the

Olympics to horn in on *their* World Cup, so they pretty much limit the men's Olympic rosters to players age twenty-three and younger, which means that the Olympics are like a junior varsity soccer championship. Wisely, the NBA wants to institute the same kind of rules for basketball. If you make the Olympics a jayvee tournament, basketball's own world championship becomes much more valuable.

But then, the most upside-down thing about the Olympic *games* is that the night they don't play *any* games at all—the opening ceremony—gets the biggest audience. More people want to watch the competitors from Paraguay and Slovenia just amble around the track in their business casual clothes than want to watch Mr. Phelps in his swim trunks.

It's equivalent to the red carpet at the Academy Awards getting a larger audience than when they actually open up the Oscar envelopes.

Simply, the Olympics are just not like other big-time sports stuff. At the Olympics, athletes talk about wanting "to medal," which is a verb that includes third place. In every other competition, the ghost of Vince Lombardi lives on, and winning is the only thing.

I guess, at the end of the day, we like the Olympics precisely because they are so different. Dare I actually say it: the Olympics are kinda, sorta innocent. Emphasis on the kinda, sorta—but still. Sometimes, in the middle of the summer it's just good enough to take a break and watch a quaint, hokey ceremony and then cheer for people you never heard of in a sport you don't care about just because . . . well, just because.

And best of all, vis-à-vis the United States, the Summer Olympics always come in our election year and give us two weeks off from the eternal campaign. Just think, if it wasn't for the Olympics, now you'd be hearing all about Rob Portman or Tim Pawlenty. Instead, you'll be hearing about Jordyn Wieber.

Who?

Heh, heh. Now you know a gymnast.

Let the opening ceremony begin.

Back in the Day

2003

Now I appreciate that many wise and sensitive citizens don't give a fig about sports, but many others the world over are devoted to them. That's the type I've wondered about. Without sports, without bowl games and the NBA and the NHL, what exactly were people doing with their time, back, say, two hundred years ago on January 1, 1803, when Thomas Jefferson sat in the White House?

Not only were there no sports to speak of then, but the president was mighty glad of it. "Games played with the ball," Mr. Jefferson declared, "are too violent for the body and stamp no character on the mind."

Of course, I am not really talking about playing games, which every culture has done with pleasure. "A man should spend his whole life at play," Plato himself opined. I'm talking about spectator sports. Oh, there have always been the occasional sports festivals like the Olympics or the fair at Nottingham where Robin Hood split the arrow, but only in the latter part of the nineteenth century did spectator games take on a quotidian aspect, did they begin to assume an everyday place in our lives. And now since television, they have simply become ubiquitous.

I remember as a child learning with wonder that at every moment of every day, a Tarzan movie was playing somewhere in the world. Well, now literally, any fan anywhere who wanted to could watch a sporting event every waking moment of every day. Plus, sports talk is constant on the radio; sports articles, statistics, betting odds fill more and more newspaper columns and periodical pages.

What did all the people who devour this stuff do before there were sports? What did they think about? What did they talk about with their buddies? They couldn't have talked about sex all the time, could they? Am I crazy to wonder about things like this? After all, it is not just sports themselves. Sports has spilled over to infect so much of the rest of our lives. Wins and losses, standings matter so much more now. Everything is ratings and polls. This is all the sportification of the world. The games are always on, always around us. What was it like, Gramps, before sports?

There, two hundred New Year's Days ago, is President Jefferson sitting in the White House, fulminating about ball games, while outside men and women are meeting each other, and none of them—none!—are talking about the Fiesta Bowl, or will the Lakers get straightened out, or who do you like in the wild card games? What were they talking about? What did involve them? What in the world filled that vacuum before sports came along?

TWO

Sports Are in the Union, Too?

2004

No one wants sports talk to be encroached upon by politics. Keep politics out of sport. Hear, hear! But, I promise you, this is not really about politics because it doesn't take sides.

And I have approached the subject gingerly, waiting until the Super Bowl is over and Janet Jackson has her shirt back on and there is nothing much else to discuss in sports except how are we going to get more goals scored in the National Hockey League.

So, here is what happened: when President Bush made his State of the Union address, he spent about half a minute deep in that invariably tedious recitation to plead with the sports universe to stop using steroids.

Ever since, the president has been lampooned for wasting our valuable time on such bric-a-brac as sport when there are so many other really crucial things for a president to bloviate about. Meryl Streep even managed to rag him about that when accepting an award at the Golden Globes. Worse, I hear about it every cocktail hour from my own beautiful and sensitive and thoughtful wife.

Well, citizens, let me come to the defense of the president. First of all, I think all presidents—and governors and bishops and college presidents and network television anchors, all muckety-mucks—have earned the right to care about a thing or two that is not necessarily at the top of the approved list of VITs—Very Important Topics.

In particular, every president in every State of the Union speech should be allowed to take a bit of time to talk about something he just happens to care about. It's a freebie, what in some games is called a bisque—a bonus you have earned the right to play whenever you choose to.

Yes, intrinsically, the environment, for example, counts more than sports, and President Bush didn't mention one word about the environment. Yes, in a perfect world, hospitals and schools count more than stadiums and parks and zoos and museums, but somehow we have to find a way to support our whole community culture. We can't rank the values of society on a David Letterman Top Ten list, and merely check them off in order as we go down the list. Life isn't that easy. Choices aren't that easy.

President Bush prefaced his remarks by saying that "athletics play such an important role in our society," and that when stars cheat with drugs, that has a particularly noxious effect on our children, on our ideals. It erodes something good. No, steroids are not terrorism or taxes or Medicare. They're not even oil drilling or global warming, but sports are something—whether or not they should be—that does have an effect upon the way many Americans think.

Also, steroids are very bad for you.

So every president should be able to take a little bit of state time to play a bisque about something that matters to him. It does not have to be about the nation United States; it can be about the society United States . . . art, drama, music, television, fashion, vacations, slot machines, pets . . . even sports.

And then, my fellow Americans, how are we to get more goals scored in the National Hockey League?

Spittin' Image

2008

During trying times such as these, I like to correspond with my friend the Duchess, the sports connoisseur, who usually sees only the grace and beauty of athletics. Unfortunately, things are so distressing now that even the sports connoisseur wishes only to discuss the ugly things she sees in sports.

"There is so much unattractiveness in games today, Frank," the Duchess began her sad missive to me. "It is only proper that we are celebrating Manny Ramirez, who, by both his demeanor and his coiffeur, represents all that is unattractive in sport today.

"I see that basketball and hockey are returning. Hockey fights are so unattractive, aren't they? And, surely, nothing is more unattractive than those droopy basketball drawers, which have been in fashion for all too long.

"Of course, nothing is so unappealing in sport as the male soccer players, who, when forming a wall before a free kick, cross their hands before their sensitive nether regions and stand there looking both unattractive and foolish, like something out of Monty Python."

But, the Duchess continued, her bile virtually boiling over, nothing upsets her so much as watching the baseball playoffs now.

"Can you explain to any person of good taste, Frank, why baseball players spit so much? It is certainly the single most unattractive thing in sport. Other athletes seldom spit, except perhaps for hockey players when they are emitting a tooth, or boxers when they are expelling blood. At least boxers have spit buckets, so-called, but baseball players spit at random, sullying all their environs.

"Yes, we can at least be grateful for small favors, that baseball players no longer expectorate tobacco. Then, dugouts looked like walk-in cuspidors.

"But regular spitting has diminished not at all. The Boston Red Sox, led by their chief sputumizer, manager Terry Francona, are surely the most promiscuous spitting team in the grand history of the national pastime.

"Why, why, why do baseball players spit so much more than all other athletes? Can't Commissioner Selig prohibit this noxious scar upon his otherwise lovely game?"

The sports connoisseur then concluded her letter with some forgotten refrains from Gilbert and Sullivan, written after they first saw a baseball game:

> *Oh the grass is green and the bases white*
> *And the players pitch and hit,*
> *But more than that, alas, alack,*
> *They only prefer to spit, to spit,*
> *They only prefer to spit.*

> *For while bowlers bowl and golfers golf*
> *And those on the ice go skate,*
> *The baseball player takes bat and glove*
> *But would rather expectorate,*
> *Would rather expectorate.*

I am the very model of a baseball star
I hit them hard and hit them far.
No, not a swimmer nor a sprinter,
Nor a skier nor a point guard, me,
For I'm lean and mean and fit as a fiddle
Ready to show the world my spittle,
Ready to show my spittle.

The Other Winnie-the-Pooh

1998

It's only midway through 1998, but already it's obvious who the athlete of the year is. It's just somewhat complicated by the fact that he's been dead for half a century. But really now, who's having a better year than Babe Ruth?

The Babe's springtime was spent being constantly recalled in Michael Jordan's reflection: Michael Jordan—the Babe Ruth of our times. The more Jordan accomplished, the more his achievements promoted Ruth—for who else was there to compare Jordan with?

And the summer—with Mark McGwire and Ken Griffey Jr. busting home runs, and the Yankees running up a stupendous record—has brought back all the special memories of that magic 1927. That was the year the Sultan of Swat hit sixty, while leading what may have been the best and the most glamorous team ever. Moreover, as the fiftieth anniversary of Ruth's death on August 16th approaches, not one, but two major documentaries—first by ESPN, then by HBO—are being aired.

It was, too, only a few years ago that another film biography was made of Ruth—even if it was pretty dreadful—a whole museum has been dedicated to the man, an *athlete*, in his native Baltimore, and as the end of the century approaches, there is no reason to think that interest in the big fellow will diminish, as every media entity assembles its official remembrance of the best of the 1900s.

The amazing thing about this continued fascination with the Babe is that there's absolutely nothing new to say. What? Is there going to be a revisionist biography of George Herman Ruth? Like any athlete of the twentieth century, his records are preserved and indisputable, and it's hardly more possible that any significant new personal history can be discovered to make us think much differently of his character. It's not exactly like reviewing anew the Jefferson presidency with some fresh material. No, there are no revelations here. Ruth was simply an amazing athlete, the savior of the national pastime, and also, coincidentally: a carouser, a perennial boy. As Paul Gallico painted him, simply and forever: "a swashbuckler built on gigantic and heroic lines." That's the whole of it, in 1928, '48, or '98.

In fact, maybe what's most continually appealing about the Babe is that it *was* all so simple. Efforts to read too much into him—as the producers tried to do in that recent biopic, starring John Goodman—simply are doomed. Obviously, the fact that the Babe's family dispatched him as a child to a quasi-reform school wounded him. So did baseball's refusal to give him a chance to manage a team, to lead other men. Yes, but also: nobody gets it all, scot-free. Ruth's was neither a particularly tragic nor complicated life.

But of all the popular cultural figures of his time—Rudolph Valentino and Paavo Nurmi, Jack Dempsey and Will Rogers, Charlie Chaplin and Sonja Henie, Marlene Dietrich and Rudy Vallee—who do we remember more than the Bambino? Well, I

can only suggest maybe Winnie-the-Pooh, another fond product of the '20s . . . but then, the bear has the advantage of going
on forever as a child.

Of course, that may be the Babe's signature, too, that
he was the most powerful child we ever had in our midst.
Maybe he is most unforgettable for that wonderfully innocent
combination—which is, coincidentally, just what America
wanted to be, itself, too, in those good old days.

Little Big Man

2014

NFL Commissioner Roger Goodell's piddling suspension of Ray Rice of the Ravens for a mere two games for his violent attack upon his fiancée has been met with shock and disappointment.

But for now: never mind Ray Rice. The larger question is whether *Goodell* is *good* enough to serve as the leader of the NFL, which is not only by far the most popular game in this country, but, in reality, something more than that. In today's divided America, what other entertainment—what other institution—means so much to many people, across all all our class, educational, racial, and ethnic spectrums?

Really, don't we need someone of greater stature at the helm of the NFL? Someone who appreciates that he should, if only symbolically, be the steward of all football in America—someone who is neither so parochial of background nor so commercially constricted as Goodell? However, he just seems to look inside out, a football dauphin who literally dreamed of being commissioner as a boy and who has worked for the league all his adult life.

Yes, to be fair, all of our major leagues now choose their leaders from within—a narrow, vocational primogeniture. But if all these so-called czars have provincial sports backgrounds, the demands upon Goodell are greater because his league casts such a longer shadow. Obviously, he is a CEO of a huge enterprise and thus must attend to the business at hand—something Goodell certainly seems to do *good enough*—but it is the power of football today that begs for a leader with greater perspective and sensitivity. Especially given the brutal nature of football that increasingly indicts it on moral charges, and the virtual drumroll of off-the-field violence—so often against women—committed by so many football players, Goodell's sideswipe of a punishment to Ray Rice indicates, if nothing else, cultural ignorance on his part.

Remember, this is a businessman who was widely compared to a tobacco executive for so long procrastinating, denying the effects of obvious occupational concussions . . . a promoter who, hang the good health of his fungible players, even now wants more Thursday games and a longer regular season schedule. But the NFL is the biggest boom this side of the Internet, so Goodell is cocooned by his ever-richer owners and a phalanx of admiring football reporters. The networks, his breathless partners, are simply bootlickers.

The exalted NFL so needs a rector, a magistrate who comes *to* the game, not from within it. It needs a leader of grace and vision. More and more Roger Goodell just looks like a slick, selling us seventy-six trombones.

Stoodint Athaleets

2010

There are certain things I simply don't believe. For example, when I see a sign that says "Aircraft Patrolling for Speeders," I don't believe it. When someone quits, saying they've become a "distraction," I don't believe it. It's because they did something wrong. I don't believe anything anybody tells me about their grandchildren. And I don't believe anything the NCAA tells me about the academic records of student-athletes. I think there is much, much more cheating in the classroom than the NCAA knows about . . . or *wants* to know about.

It's the old business of garbage in/garbage out. The various colleges—which is to say, the various athletic departments—report grades to the NCAA, which accepts them prima facie. How can the NCAA ever tell if some stooge is taking a test for an athlete; if some tutor is writing a term paper for an athlete; if some professor is dishing out passing grades to the failing athletes he cheers for?

As Bob Knight, the retired basketball coach, says: If the NCAA had been in charge of Normandy, we would've attacked Greece, and given our soldiers all the wrong ammunition.

Consider the way the most recent academic scandal, at the University of North Carolina, was, shall we *generously* say, uncovered. The NCAA was investigating more obvious charges, that the Tar Heel players were dealing with agents, when it just blindly stumbled across the internal classroom shenanigans. And last week, it was a newspaper, the *Birmingham News*, that uncovered the fact that a Kentucky basketball player, Eric Bledsoe, had gotten into school with a doctored transcript.

We could expect academic monkey business at Kentucky, because the basketball coach there, John Calipari, has already skipped out of two other colleges after serious violations scarred the programs on his watch, but the Carolina revelations are the more distressing because it is one of the finest state universities in the nation. Even the bleeding hearts among us can only conclude that if they're cheating at Chapel Hill, athletic academic fraud must be truly commonplace.

"Look," a Division I athletic director tells me candidly, "any big college, you can hide players, you can hide stuff."

Saddest of all, when some courageous academics have dared blow the whistle—at places like Tennessee, Ohio State, and Minnesota—they've all too often been castigated as tattletales. *Hey, professor, get on our team.*

I'll never forget a tutor from a big-time school literally crying on the phone to me as he confessed to his part in the corruption of athletics as students. He felt especially ashamed because it was his alma mater. "They tell me everybody does it," he said. "Is that really true?"

If it makes you feel any better, I replied, yeah, probably—probably just about everybody. There are no referees in big-time college classrooms.

The Real Bad Guys

2007

Periodically now, a former professional player, who nobody ever heard of when he was playing, comes out with a book revealing that he is gay. The latest is John Amaechi, late of the NBA. Each account invariably details the difficulty the player had in keeping his secret in the midst of such a macho culture.

Then, following that, there is the inevitable response, which is to show compassion for what the gay athlete endured while castigating his league for being so homophobic a culture. Now please understand, I could not be more sympathetic with gay players like Amaechi. I can only imagine how painfully difficult it must be to live and play in such a competitive environment while having every day to pretend to be something that you are not.

I would also acknowledge that any group of young men— yes, especially those in athletics, where the testosterone is boiling—will be generally rude and insensitive. It's not nice but it has surely come with the territory ever since young men foregathered to go out hunting for wild woolly mammoths.

I can quite understand how poor Amaechi had to steel himself not to cringe almost every day in the locker room, listening to random gay bashing, hearing every mean epithet ever

employed for homosexuals. But hey, a lot of that is just brag-
gadocio and posturing, and a lot of it comes from a relatively
small percentage of any team.

When, to use an analogy, women reporters first were allowed in locker rooms a generation ago, most of the players
accommodated themselves. It was only a handful on any team
that found gross and sophomoric ways to behave.

Yes, there are jerks on every team and a few outright homo-
phobes. But my experience and instinct lead me to believe that
if a professional male athlete did dare come out, most of his
teammates would accept it and the predominant peer pressure
would force the numbskulls to go along.

Evidence? Well, okay. I know personally and well two absolutely outstanding athletes who were stars for many years—one
in a team sport, one in an individual sport. No, neither ever
came out. But yes, everybody knew they were gay. But they
were good guys and the one team player was a fabulous team-
mate. And so, after a while it just wasn't an issue.

So I believe that the reason gay male athletes stay in the
closet has far more to do with the public than with the locker
room. Especially in our society today where you find so much
incivility in the grandstand, what player would dare risk giving the beered-up Neanderthal creeps a chance to scream vile,
personal insults every time he missed the basket or struck out?

Isn't it revealing that not a single American leading man
actor has ever admitted his homosexuality when he was still
a star? And yet we all know that the theater is institutionally
welcoming to gays. Obviously, it is the fear of the audience,
not of their colleagues, that keeps gay actors playing straight.

Male athletes can be boors and bullies, you bet. Teams
and leagues themselves can be hidebound. Yes, granted: professional sports is not the most forgiving environment. But to

hear every time a former athlete comes out that players are especially prejudiced is simply a canard. The villains are much more the ones cheering and booing than the ones playing. The bad guys are us.

An update:

Since I wrote this almost a decade ago, I think the experience of Michael Sam and Jason Collins (in their brief appearances in the big leagues of sport as acknowledged homosexuals) has shown what I wrote then, that gay athletes can indeed be accepted in the locker room. They suffered no enmity in the locker room, and were, in fact, rather casually accepted.

However, I also think that we've seen society change sufficiently that whenever we do get a prominent gay player, he will not suffer harshly from the crowds, as I speculated in 2007. Any fan who acted crudely toward a known gay athlete today would himself have to endure the wrath of other fans. I'm positive now there's a greater tolerance toward gays in the grandstand, as there is everywhere else.

Also note that just since 2007 it has become fairly common for actors to casually let on that they're gay. That in itself reflects the great change in the public's thinking on the subject.

On the other hand, I'm suspicious of the glib assumption often advanced that we must accept the fact that there must be as high a percentage of gay males in sports as in the whole population. As a rule, birds of a feather do flock together, and in the past—emphasis on the past—when there was more homophobia in sport, I suspect that some potentially fine athletes turned away from sport. Likewise, where there was a more accepting attitude, as in ballet, we were never surprised that a disproportionate number of gay men took up dance.

The Volunteer State

2013

I read the other day that sixteen thousand people have been recruited as volunteers for next year's Super Bowl in New Jersey, and suddenly it occurred to me: the Super Bowl is one of the great financial bonanzas of modern times. From the players to the networks to the hotels, everybody involved with it makes a killing. Why would anybody volunteer to work for free for the Super Bowl? Would you volunteer to work free for Netflix or Disney World?

Apparently, though, there are more chumps in the Garden State than we see on television's *Jersey Shore* or hear about in the Rutgers Athletic Department.

I mean, if you want to volunteer, there are so many things that could really use your help. Like hospitals and schools and churches and museums and libraries and all sorts of wonderful charities. *Why would anybody volunteer for the Super Bowl?*

Of course, golf and tennis tournaments, where the players and promoters make hundreds of thousands of dollars, have been getting suckers to volunteer for years. It's amazing how sports seduce us fans.

We can take some comfort in knowing that it's not just American citizens who are such easy marks. Whole cities and countries throw themselves at sports. Most recently, no doubt you've heard about the riots in Rio de Janeiro, where the Brazilian people are a little put out that while such things as food, medicine, and shelter may be hard to come by, the government has put up billions for both the World Cup next summer and the Summer Olympics in 2016.

The Brazilian sports honorarium pales before what the Russians are laying out for next winter's Olympics, though: a record $50 billion, which is only $38 billion more than the original bid proposal. Sports events always cost a tad more than the officials, who desperately want the event, uh, estimate. And the Olympics and World Cup always lead cities and countries on by saying that the infrastructure built for their games will be a long-term boon for the country. Like Greece, which, as you know, has been living high on the hog ever since Athens overspent for the 2004 Olympics.

But there's always a new sucker somewhere out there. The Olympics and the World Cup scramble to find novel places to go. Like the 2022 soccer championship will be in Qatar, where it is known to be too hot for soccer. Or next year's Winter Olympics in Sochi, where it seldom gets to be winter. They have stockpiled snow there. All of Russia, suburban Siberia, and they pick a place where you have to save snow?

But, if you've got the money, the Olympics and the World Cup will be only too happy to come on over and enjoy the facilities you've built just for them. Oh my, what we all do for sports.

Why would anybody volunteer to work for free for the Super Bowl?

An update:
That familiar old preface we so often hear—usually from long-winded people—is: "To make a long story short." I've noticed lately that that

expression has become more common, but, to make a long story short, it's been shortened to just "long story short." I'll even bet it's gotten initialed in the text universe to LSS.

Well, long story short, last year I was astonished to discover that guileless fans were actually volunteering their services, for free, gratis, to the Super Bowl—which, of course, makes a gazillion million dollars for the NFL and its gracious owners. I want you to keep in mind, too, that the NFL is officially a nonprofit, even though commissioner Roger Goodell makes in excess of $40 million a year. Lord knows what they'd pay him if he was doing a good job.

Now the 2018 Super Bowl has been awarded to Minneapolis, and thanks to superb investigative work by the Minneapolis Star-Tribune, a 153-page list of stipulations that the league demanded has been revealed. Here are just some of the demands for what is trumpeted as "America's unofficial holiday": The league gets every cent of ticket revenue; thirty-five thousand free parking spaces; free ads in local newspapers and on radio stations, and lots of free billboards (just so we'll know the Super Bowl is in town); and free presidential suites in the top hotels. Further, all ATMs at the stadium must be affiliated with NFL-approved credit cards. If cell phone reception isn't quite good enough, then Minneapolis has to build the NFL sufficient new cell phone towers. The NFL even unsuccessfully tried to demand the right to select the only vendors at the airport—the public airport—who could sell NFL merchandise.

And the greed goes on and on. Worth keeping in mind, too, is the fact that the new Minneapolis stadium is costing about $500 million in taxpayer money with a sweetheart deal for the owners, who were recently called out for "racketeering" and "rob(bing) their partners" by a judge in a New Jersey case. NFL owners are such munificent citizens. The NFL now is also thinking about forcing halftime Super

Bowl acts to pay for the privilege of appearing. Have these people no shame?

Long story short. Last year I said I was amazed that anybody would volunteer for the NFL. Now, it's simple to declare: If you ever volunteer for the Super Bowl, you're suckers.

L . . . S . . . S.

THREE

The Pursuit
of Sports

2001

Some thoughts about sports in these United States of America on the occasion of this first Independence Day of this new century:

When in the course of human events . . .

At the time when that was written, 225 years ago, human events never involved big games. There were no Wimbledon quarterfinals, no Firecracker 500.

Life, liberty and the pursuit of happiness . . .

Certainly, though, sports are now very much a part of that pursuit. It's also a reflection of the liberty we enjoy. After all, traditionally, those among us with the least opportunity, but with genuine talent, have possessed, with sport, the fairest path to success.

We hold these truths to be self-evident, that all men are created equal . . .

At last women too have been granted the freedom to play sports in this favored land. Yet . . . yet curiously, while sports are the most democratic of endeavors, it is, on this Independence Day, worth remembering that of those Americans with talent, athletes have enjoyed the least independence.

So often American sports have been run in an arbitrary and unfair manner, with a long history of tyranny. Certainly, no institutional legislation in America has been more in conflict with freedom than the so-called reserve clause, which, for decades, bound professional players in all major team sports to franchises against their will.

Moreover, our amateur federations have been despotic fiefdoms. The NCAA remains yet a shameless autocracy where the college players are essentially indentured servants, refused compensation for their labors, and otherwise held in an onerous peonage that arbitrarily denies them their freedoms.

But there is much to be said for the way that we Americans cheer. Unlike most all other nations of the world, we do not place an emphasis upon our national teams. We do not need sports to exercise pride in our country. No, we are no less fervent in our allegiances, but by cheering for the teams of our particular cities or our schools, rather than for our whole national self, we defuse foolish jingoistic passion.

It's only right, too, that in a heterogeneous society, we have many more popular sports and many more teams to choose from.

And yes, we may complain about bad decisions, but we accept them better than most.

Instant replay helps. Except perhaps for obstreperous, inebriated college boys looking for an excuse to be obstreperous, inebriated college boys, we rarely express our sporting displeasure by rioting. Ironically, if we are more violent away from the arena than other people, we are not so wild at the games. We learn to be decent sports, playing the game or watching it, better than most.

And . . . with a firm reliance on the protection of divine providence, we mutually pledge to each other our lives, our fortunes, and our sacred honor to have another beer, please, and a hot dog and some peanuts and a carefree Independence Day at the game of your choice.

Baseball's Sad Lexicon

2010

It was one hundred years ago when Franklin P. Adams wrote what is, after "Casey at the Bat," sports' most famous poem. It appeared in the *New York Evening Mail*, titled "Baseball's Sad Lexicon," as Adams lamented how three players on the Chicago Cubs kept thwarting his beloved hometown team.

It went, of course, like this:

These are the saddest of possible words:
"Tinker to Evers to Chance."
Trio of bear cubs, fleeter than birds,
Tinker and Evers and Chance.
Ruthlessly pricking our gonfalon bubble,
Making a Giant hit into a double—
Words that are heavy with nothing but trouble:
"Tinker to Evers to Chance."

The three gentlemen who were upsetting the sports-page poet in 1910 were the double-play combination of Joe Tinker,

Johnny Evers, and Frank Chance. But today, a century later, in 2010, all baseball faces a much more serious scourge—the dreadful strategy of what is called "working the count."

That means that the idea is no longer to swing away, but to fight a battle of attrition, make the pitcher throw more pitches, stall, wait him out.

So the pitcher retaliates by taking more time and the catcher makes serial trips to the mound, and the batters call time out constantly, incessantly monkeying with their batting gloves, delaying, loitering, dragging out every at bat. Hitters who can take pitches and get walks now seem more valued than hitters who can actually . . . hit.

Come back, steroids: all is forgiven.

So the games get longer. The average time now approaches three hours. Our hero is Cowboy Joe West, an umpire who dared publicly call out the Yankees and Red Sox for being the worst offenders—which they are, year after year.

The Yankees' old manager, Joe Torre, has carried the virus to his new team, the Dodgers. Now L.A. is the slowest team in the National League . . . working the count.

And, of course, we spectators are the big losers, down for the count.

Defenders of baseball always get very sensitive when critics snort that the game is too slow. Yes, part of baseball's charm is that by taking its time, it enjoys an intellectual suspense other sports don't. A slow dance is more romantic.

At a certain point, though, the obsession for working the count is twisting the game's cherished rhythm into stultifying sluggishness.

And so, a century on from Tinker to Evers to Chance, we have, this year, "Baseball's Sadder Lexicon":

These are the saddest of possible words:
"Working the count."
Hopelessly boring, slower than curds,
Working the count.
Strategically destroying the grace of the game,
Turning each at bat into a pain,
Words that are heavy with nothing but shame:
"Working the count."

To an Athlete Leaving Young

2012

Now that Tim Tebow is out of hearts and minds, and we can actually turn our attention to other things, let us go clear to the other side of the world. There, a short while ago, while preparing for the Australian Open, Serena Williams said: "I don't love tennis today, but . . . I've actually never liked sports."

While her confession might have surprised some, I suspect that even more fans were irritated, actually angered, that an athlete—a great champion!—could utter such blasphemy.

We sometimes also hear the sentiment that we'd like to see an athlete quit near the peak of his career, but when Tiki Barber, the running back, did just that a few years ago, he was utterly astonished at the reaction of so many fans. They all but berated him—*how dare you leave the game!*

It's not just that so many of us love sports so and can't comprehend someone who's in the game not caring for it all that much. Rather, I think, there's a lot of envy involved.

So many people—girls as well as boys now—grow up playing sports and loving them and ultimately failing at them; and so when we see someone who achieved what we couldn't, we're all the more put out if they can blithely turn their back on it.

Why, fans have even been shocked at the recent revelations that several ice hockey goons really didn't enjoy being goons.

Now, when somebody from another glamorous profession —an actor, say, or a model—walks away from success, there isn't the same intensity of either jealousy or bafflement because not so many of us tried to act or model when we were growing up. Ahh, but how many of us kids played sports and dreamed of being a star?

The irony is, in my experience, that for those athletes who do make it to the top, a passion for the game does not necessarily best light that path to glory.

In fact, at the age of thirty, Serena is old for a tennis player, and she may still be a contender only because she has not loved tennis so much. Through the years, it's aggravated a lot of people in her sport when she's appeared cavalier about the very thing that has brought her fame and fortune, but the simple fact that she has been able to distance herself and find other outlets may explain why she's not yet burned out, physically or emotionally.

On the other hand, it's also my experience that a lot of the more restrained athletes who do quit before they are done find out only afterward how much the game really meant to them.

When Tiki Barber wanted desperately to come back after five seasons, nobody wanted him. Youth may be wasted on the young, but in sports, the most telling truth is that youth must not be wasted.

The All-Purpose Sports Movie

2006

Really, do we need another *Rocky* movie? Perhaps this time Sylvester Stallone will be fighting for the AARP title. But I don't want to pick on *Rocky*. All sports movies, including, I might say, a couple I've written myself, are exactly the same. It doesn't make any difference—boxing, horse racing, baseball, football, basketball, hockey, you name it; they're all the same.

And so to save you the trouble of ever having to go see another sports movie, here, just for you, is your one-size-fits-all sports movie script.

Act I: The introduction of hopelessness.

You are the sorriest excuse for a team I've ever coached. I quit!

Listen, muffin, I know how much you love Blue Comet. But face it, honey, no horse has ever run in the Derby with a prosthetic leg before.

Act II: Hope arrives in a surprise package.

Sure, Bunky is an old drunk and a lot of people think the game has passed him by. But if anybody can make a winner, it's Bunky. What do you say? Give him a chance?

Okay, Coach.

All right, Daddy.

What have I got to lose if I want to be the champ?

Act III: Unusual strategy.

Okay, team, here's what we're going to do. I remember this formation from back in '72 when I was coaching State U. If it was good enough then, it'll work now if you trust me. You got trouble with that, Mickey?

Blue Comet loves ya, muffin. That means he'll run his best if we put a girl jockey on him. Ginger don't want to be a stripper no more. Here's her chance to show she can do what she really loves.

I know you don't want to see KO hurt, Blanche. Even if he's losing his eyesight, let him have that one more shot at the title.

Act IV: The climactic contest

Hey, guys, I don't care what the experts say. We can win. And Mickey, all right, you showed me you care enough about the team and not just yourself. I'm putting you back in the starting lineup.

Ginger, Blue Comet can't read the odds board. He don't know he's a hundred to one. Let them other horses fight over the lead. But when you hit the quarter pole, then just hang on for dear life.

Never mind what they say, KO. It ain't fists going to win this fight; it's heart. And I wouldn't trade yours for no valentine in the world.

Act V: Finally, of course, victory.

There's no time left on the clock. Throw it, Mickey! Throw it! Yeah, he got it! You guys won the Rose Bowl!

No, coach, *we* won the Rose Bowl.

Here she comes, muffin! She's flying now! Come on Blue Comet! Come on Blue Comet! One more jump! Yeah, yeah! He won the Derby, muffin!

No, Mr. Bunky, *we* won the Derby.

Eight . . . Nine . . . Ten . . . You did it, KO! You did it! You're the champ!

No, Bunky, *we're* the champs, together.

The sequel, *The Champ Returns*, will open next week.

The Other Sports Violence

2003

Athletes have always been perceived as ladies' men. They were the modern version of the strong and silent cowboy. The vision of the star quarterback standing with his arm around the beautiful strawberry blond cheerleader is embedded in our romantic mythology. Likewise, it's always been understood that on the road, athletes are tomcats. Oh, yeah, booze and broads. That was the athletic liturgy.

But the playing around used to be framed in a comic, almost antic fashion. How many knee-slapping tales were told of the handsome hero who could carouse till the wee hours, stagger back to the hotel with a gorgeous prize, then somehow emerge sleepless and hungover only to lead his team to victory? Jim Bouton's accounts in his memoir, *Ball Four,* thirty years ago—ballplayers drinking and philandering—may have shocked the more guileless fans at the time, but even then the players' nocturnal high jinks struck more of a fraternity house chord. "Boys will be boys," unless, of course, you were married to one of the boys.

Obviously, the sex lives of athletes were never quite so benign as the pleasant legends had it. But still, at some point in recent years, something changed. Rakishness turned into ravishment. Hardly a week goes by, it seems, without some pro or college star being hauled up on some charge of brutality against a woman. It's risky to try to explain this simply, but certainly part of the sorry trend can be accounted for by the fact that athletes are now given so much and forgiven so much and from so early on that they become imbued with a sense of entitlement previously found only in royal princes of the realm.

After a while, it's hard to believe that anybody will turn you down, particularly any woman. Yet, while there is a lot of moaning about the athletes' violence toward women, has it affected the popularity of any sport, especially in the NBA, where misconduct of all kinds appears most abundant? Well, when you hear fans complain about sports today, the complaints deal with ticket prices and the players don't care that much and they're not loyal to their team and they make too much money. But never do I hear anybody say, "Well, I don't want to go to games because those guys are pigs."

In the extreme case of Mike Tyson, the box office appeal even seems to have increased since his rape conviction. In other words, the lesson we keep hearing is that what athletes do to women, no matter how awful, that doesn't involve their sport itself doesn't matter.

In this latest case, most of the speculation has revolved around whether or not Kobe Bryant's endorsement contracts would be damaged by a possible guilty verdict on the charge of sexual assault. Nobody has much bothered to contemplate if his behavior would have any adverse effect on the NBA's popularity. Evidently, products are more sensitive than fans. Until we see evidence to the contrary, we can continue to assume that how pro athletes treat women is simply not germane so long as they treat the games we love with respect and devotion.

An update:
The fact that I wrote this in 2003 shows how the ingrained atti-tude about it being rather acceptable for athletes to take advantage of women prevailed into this century. No wonder so many men in sports were taken aback when, rather suddenly, offensive sexual behavior was no longer tolerated.

Another Way to Win

2012

When last we left the NCAA, it was February madness; colleges were jumping conferences, suing each other; coaches were claiming rivals had cheated in recruiting—the usual nobility of college sports.

And then, in the midst of all this, the men's basketball team at Washington College of Chestertown, Maryland, journeyed to Pennsylvania to play Gettysburg College in a Division-III Centennial Conference game.

It was senior night, and the loudest cheers went to Cory Weissman, number three, five feet eleven inches, a team captain—especially when he walked out onto the court as one of Gettysburg's starting five.

Yes, he was a captain, but it was, you see, the first start of his college career. Cory had played a few minutes on the varsity as a freshman, never even scoring. But then, after that season, although he was only eighteen years old, he suffered a major stroke. He was unable to walk for two weeks. His whole left side was paralyzed. He lost his memory, had seizures.

But by strenuously devoting himself to his rehabilitation, Cory slowly began to improve. He was able to return to college, and by this year, he could walk without a limp and even participated in the pregame layup drills.

So for senior night, against Washington, his coach, George Petrie, made the decision to start Cory. Yes, he would play only a token few seconds, but it meant a great deal to Cory and to Gettysburg. All the more touching, the Washington players stood and cheered him.

That was supposed to be the end of it, but with Gettysburg ahead by a large margin and less than a minute left in the game, Coach Petrie sent Cory back in.

Nobody could understand, though, what happened next, why the Washington coach, Rob Nugent, bothered to call time out. The fans didn't know what he told his players there in the huddle: that as quickly as they could, they should foul number three. And one of them did. And with seventeen seconds left, Cory Weissman strode to the free-throw line. He had two shots.

Suddenly, the crowd understood what Coach Nugent had sought to do. There was not a sound in the gym. Cory took the ball and shot. It drifted to the left, missing disastrously. The crowd stirred. The referee gave Cory the ball back. He eyed the rim. He dipped and shot. The ball left his hand and flew true. Swish. All net.

The crowd cried as much as it cheered.

The assistant vice president for athletics at Gettysburg, David Wright, wrote to Washington College: "Your coach, Rob Nugent, along with his staff and student-athletes, displayed a measure of compassion that I have never witnessed in over thirty years of involvement in intercollegiate athletics."

Cory Weissman had made a point.

Washington College had made an even larger one.

Par for the Course

2006

The *New York Times* recently revealed—on page one, no less—that John Mack—the head of Morgan Stanley—was stocking up his board of directors with golfing buddies.

Now, first of all, I hate to be the one to tell the *Times*, but this goes under the heading of: Dog Bites Man. It's always been my understanding that you can't either (a) work on Wall Street or (b) qualify for a board of directors, unless you do play golf.

But, upon reflection, I appreciate the newspaper of record for bringing this gross social injustice to our attention. This is a diverse nation and we make an effort to see that our boards and executive suites are open to both sexes; to men and women of all races, religions, and ethnic origins. Surely, it is time to expect the same sort of diversification of our sporting persuasions.

I don't know about you, but I fear for a nation's economy that is so dominated by golfers and their cozy links mentality. It's just a vicious circle: from the tee to the nineteenth hole to the boardroom. I say, let's get some bowlers making command decisions.

For example, the *Times* article quoted the boss of another investment bank, defending Mr. Mack's penchant for isolating himself with golfers, by saying: A CEO wants a guy with shared experience and values. A guy, say, who gives him putts within three feet.

Whoa, there! Fore! Was this country built on that attitude? I don't think so! I don't think your Jay Goulds, your J. P. Morgans, your John Jacob Astors carved out empires by expecting their adversaries to provide them with gimmes. In point of fact, I suspect that it is precisely this you-scratch-my-back, I'll-scratch-yours disposition which accounts for the fact that China just about owns us today. Somehow I don't think the boys in Shanghai and Guangzhou are letting everybody off the hook so easily. They're saying, Putt that sucker out, buster.

The trouble with golf is that you're not really competing against your opponent. It's just you versus the course. The competition is internal. I want my money in the hands of some mano-a-mano guys: some tennis players, squash players, racquetball players; hard-boiled competitors who pound that ball right back at you, who want to win six–love, six–love. No mulligans out there! No short-selling! No, sir! That's the American way.

And what does everybody have in golf? A handicap, right? *Golf Digest* magazine actually ranks American executives by their handicaps. And what's the point of handicaps? To make everyone equal. Golf is the only game where the weak are propped up and the strong, penalized. Which, of course, is why so many people play it—there being a lot more weak sisters around than top dogs.

In fact, if you really think about it, golf is very socialistic. If golf were a country, it would be Cuba. That fuzzy thinking may be the greatest threat to our dear capitalistic way of life. It behooves all of you to go to stockholder meetings and demand full disclosure, about the golf syndicate that rules our company.

FOUR

The Super Bard

2008

The Super Bowl has grown so big that National Public Radio could think of only one man to cover it: William Shakespeare. The Bard was in Arizona when the two teams met the media, whereupon The Bard filed this exclusive play.

The Players
Sideline Wench, a reporter for the Duchy of Fox; Kornheisercranz, herald; Wilbonstern, herald; Brady, a fair-haired boy; Eli, a boy; reporters, bloggers, correspondents, cameramen, soundmen, hangers-on, sycophants, small children throwing rose petals, et al.

Act One: Scene One

Our drama begins as a slovenly mob of sports journalists enters the field at the University of Phoenix stadium. A fetching reporter, the Sideline Wench of the Duchy of Fox, steps forward.

SIDELINE WENCH: Since none of my sex 'tis allowed
Within the network booth on high,
'Twill be my one sweet distaff voice
Midst these growling sports-page lowlifes

Which will, upon my sideline nunnery,
Dare confront the pretty Brady.

Two heralds, Kornheisercranz and Wilbonstern, wearing hideous matching ESPN doublets, elbow the Sideline Wench aside.

KORNHEISERCRANZ: Upon this line-ed greensward set within
A desert the Almighty fixed but for cactus
Will be this, our strange stage for Sabbath's pigskin war,
Waged by mesomorphs come from green Blue States afar.

WILBONSTERN: 'Tis stranger still the warrior names affixed,
For they would better be the one, the other.
Think on it: those called Giants are but dwarfs here,
Mere ciphers in the point spread, a goodly dozen down.

KORNHEISERCRANZ: Yea, the true giants, these peerless
    monsters,
Call themselves Patriots, e'en though they give shame
To that sweet address, trafficking more as traitors,
Scoundrels in video deceit, cashing all manner of Belichicks.

SIDELINE WENCH: But, hush all you scribes who bloviate so,
For comes now fair Brady, he who is as super
In his mortal company as e're this game is to sport.
But soft! Let me look upon him as if I filled his embrace.
Oh! A visage that Narcissus would have traded for!
And a manner that knows neither pressure nor fear.
But, alas, 'tis women of fashion that he favors,
For one already has his babe, another his flowers,
And I, only a sideline wench who can but model dreams.

And now Brady enters amid a crowd of admirers. Small children toss rose petals in his path.

KORNHEISERCRANZ: Methinks the crunch upon his presence
  is so great,
And the paparazzi do shine forth such a spangled glare
That the great golden orb above must be dimmed
And the sounds of Niagara itself seem noiseless
Before the din of questions that confront our great Brady.

THE MEDIA: Brady, Brady, what is afoot with thee?

BRADY: Good men of the press box, I come whole to you,
For always the feats I have achieved were upon my two feet.
And Sunday, I shall play the same no less,
One game at a time, one good foot before the other.
But now, I bid you, let me take my leave to join my mates,
For by rolling alone, there is no way for Moss to gather
passes.

NARRATOR (*in hushed tones*): And so Brady exits stage left . . .
  and the heralds return.

WILBONSTERN: But look now, who approaches from yon
  other way?
'Tis young Eli, who seems, in his manner, yet a boy,
No match for such a paragon as the dauntless Brady.

KORNHEISERCRANZ: 'Tis so, he is yet more Manning than
  man,
But the football blood that fills that callow vessel
Is as royal as Brady ever bought to his captured throne.
Eli is the seed of the sainted Archie
And thus branch from the same tree as Peyton,
He, who made stallions of Colts but twelvemonth past.
Mayhap the lad can, with a pigskin, find the same mark
Little David did when bookies of yore favored huge Goliath.

SIDELINE WENCH: So, withal, is the grandeur of Brady match for the legacy of Eli?

Forsooth . . .

With that I take to silence and send it back up to the big boys in the booth.

Worse Even Than Us?

2010

As sure as death and no new taxes, American sports fans are always convinced that the people who run sports here are dimwits. Well, yes, we have occasionally had some real nincompoops in charge of various professional American sports, and not even Pericles could successfully manage the NCAA, but in point of fact, our domestic sports are a paragon of efficiency and integrity compared with the way international athletic organizations are managed.

The latest global sports embarrassment is FIFA, the genteel soccer-mob syndicate, which, in the face of massive transparent corruption, has reelected, unchallenged, its seventy-five-year-old president, who says it's better to keep these naughty little infractions in the bosom of the football family. "Hear! Hear!" cried the executive committee, some of whom seem to value honor so highly that they leave it to the possession of others.

And we've also been treated to the scandalous antics of the International Olympic Committee and the ludicrous jingoistic judges' scoring of the International Skating Union and the International Cycling Union, which somehow couldn't see that the entire sport had turned into a drugstore, and on and on and on.

The general problem with international athletic federations is that they're simply too unwieldy—too many cultures in too many countries. They're both ethically and organizationally a Tower of Babel. Moreover, because sports are a good-time thing, these organizations, in all nations, tend to attract second-rate people. The better types of volunteers are more likely to work for issues more important to humankind: boring things like health and hunger, peace and justice, for example.

As a consequence, international sports federations are stocked with flimsy people who like the fun and games, and so it's rather easy for someone who's a bit more wily, willing to devote himself to the internal politics, to be able to rise up and become a little tin-pot dictator—Exhibit A being Sepp Blatter, the shopworn FIFA potentate.

At least team sports, like soccer, have some base structure, with organized leagues and associations. By contrast, individual sports rather take as their model Somalia. Eternally, innocents cry out that if sports like boxing and tennis could only have a "czar," then world order would reign. But that's simply pie-in-the-sky whimsy when it comes to a global amusement park where agents and promoters and other self-interested warlords ride the range.

Soccer also has its own special problem. It's so popular throughout the world that nobody wants to risk losing FIFA's favor. OMG! OMG! No football! As with all political machines, tribute is paid and bliss is ensured by feigning ignorance.

Where Have We Gone?

1999

It was really quite extraordinary—wasn't it?—how much attention was paid to the old man as he lay dying a few months ago. As if he were some great head of state, bulletins were issued, regularly, as he came into and out of a coma, on and off life support, as the priests and his relatives arrived to bid him good-bye.

Blessedly, he's out of the hospital now, but his close call still raises the question: Why does Joe DiMaggio merit so much of our attention? Why do we care so?

Oh, no doubt he was a superb ballplayer, one of the best. But just in his own era most experts rank Ted Williams above him; some, Stan Musial, as well. Willie Mays invariably surpasses DiMaggio as the finest center fielder ever. No, great talent as he was, DiMaggio is more cultural a figure than he is merely athletic.

He represents very well, I think, a place and a moment—the fabled New York City of the middle of the century. The only time we ever had an Oz in America. We can still see young Mr. DiMaggio in one of his rich, sleek suits, with a cigarette and a martini at a supper club, just as well as we remember him in his pinstripes, elegantly patrolling—*patrolling*, that wonderful outfield word—the great green expanse of Yankee Stadium. Indeed, as bizarre a pairing as it is, the only two men of our times whom I picture always wearing a suit—always—are Joe DiMaggio and Richard Nixon.

The Yankee Clipper wore his somewhat better.

The Yankee Clipper. Not a nickname. Oh, God no. More a title. DiMaggio was *the* Yankee in those last years when the Bronx Bombers absolutely ruled baseball, and when baseball itself was still, undisputed, the national pastime. So not only does DiMaggio evoke the New York of a certain postwar time, when there were no chain stores, no malls, no suburbs, no rock 'n' roll; he also best represents those last years when baseball ruled supreme.

Ironically, while Paul Simon used DiMaggio's name as an afterthought because it scanned so much better for his song lyric than did "Mickey Mantle," Simon stumbled upon the truth. DiMaggio was the symbol of an era; Mantle wasn't. *Where have you gone, Joe DiMaggio?* asks where has the past gone. Where have *we* gone?

But, curiously, DiMaggio's been forgotten for what matters most in his legend—that he was a significant ethnic figure. Not quite as Jackie Robinson was, nor as Roberto Clemente, but as the first great American star of Italian heritage. Twenty-five thousand Italian Americans came out to Yankee Stadium that day in 1936 when DiMaggio debuted.

Maybe because DiMaggio was a high school dropout, originally simply called "Dago" by his teammates, maybe for that reason he was always insecure in the larger world—so retiring and distant, mysterious even. And maybe because Italians in America are no longer systematically discriminated against, as they were then, it's easier to forget what DiMaggio endured and how he mattered most under pressure. But long ago we stopped asking: *Where did you come from, Joe DiMaggio?* And that's good.

Finally, too, I think it counted less that he married Marilyn Monroe than that their marriage didn't last. The most beautiful movie star in the world and the most graceful athlete—the perfect physical union for our age, the best since Venus and Adonis—but even they couldn't make it work.

We, as imperfect human beings, took some naturally mean-spirited comfort from thinking that even the gods and goddesses can fail, too. It is the tragedy of the hero that yet enthralls us as much as the glamour ever did.

Me and Paul

2008

There's an old French expression: "An actress is a little more than a woman, and an actor is a little less than a man."

No one ever thought that of Paul Newman. In a way, men and women alike saw him more as a hero than an actor.

Certainly, it's hard to think of anyone else in show business who had as many sports connections as Newman did. He was the decathlete of Hollywood. You read the tributes to him, and people from various disparate sports all write about him so fondly, all crediting him with helping their sport.

Of course, Newman's connection to automobile racing was real, not celluloid. He was an authentically outstanding driver. He loved the sport so much.

Newman made a point of going back to Indianapolis this past May to see the trials for the 500, one last time. I guess it was his way of taking the checkered flag, holding it out the window, and doing one more victory lap.

But as race people embraced him as their own, ice hockey people adored him for his performance in *Slap Shot*. That movie was such a boon to hockey, just as he made pool more glamorous, playing Fast Eddie Felson in *The Hustler* and then in *The Color of Money*.

If Paul Newman was connected, it must be good.

Now, I happen to live in Westport, Connecticut, where he was absolutely beloved, as a citizen, as a neighbor. Oh my, how we've always loved to say that we lived in the same town as Paul Newman. What a cachet that's always been!

Of course, we're supposed to be sophisticated in Westport, so the rule was you didn't make a fuss when you saw him around. But, of course, people kept watching him out of the corner of their eyes.

One time, years ago, when he was still indisputably the handsomest man in the world, my wife ran across him in a bookstore. All the other women were pretending not to notice, bumping into the shelves.

Newman was with one of his daughters. At the checkout counter, he called over to her, "Okay, honey, let's go."

And, my wife says, every woman in that store—including my wife, I'm sure—gave an involuntary head feint toward the door. I'm sure it was better than watching a vaudeville sketch.

The last time I saw him was a few months ago. There were already rumors that he was dying. He was never so large as he appeared on the screen—but now, even as he was still in good humor, he looked positively frail.

We were at a small concert and, just by chance, he and his wife, Joanne Woodward, sat right next to me and my wife.

When the lights dimmed, I happened to glance over, and I saw that, right away, he'd taken Joanne's hand. They'd only been married fifty years. He kept holding her hand all the way through, just like they were teenagers.

I reached over and took my wife's hand. There are not many things any of us could do so well as Paul Newman, but, I thought, if you could follow his lead in any way, then you'd be a fool not to.

Bad Bubbly

2005

Let us, this morning, contemplate style and etiquette, two—I'm afraid—elements sorely lacking in sport today. To begin with, celebrations. If you've been watching any of the baseball play-offs, you're only too aware that when a team clinches victory, it immediately proceeds to the clubhouse, where all the players thereupon act like total jackasses, spraying champagne all over one another and any interlopers foolish enough to enter the premises.

When did this asinine exercise start? I know champagne is a celebratory beverage, but the idea is, well, yes, to drink it. Yes, a bit of the bubbly may spray forth when the cork pops, but champagne is to be imbibed. That's why it comes in bottles. You know what these forced exhibitions of gaiety remind me of? How many times have you been to a wedding reception, and when the cake is cut, the bride takes a piece of cake and smashes it into the groom's face? The first bride who did this—what, fifty years ago?—was original; now, not funny.

To make it all the more ridiculous, now sheets of plastic are put up in the locker room before the postgame jubilee to protect clothes from the champagne storms. So it seems even more contrived. Oh, well, it's not as stylized as the football rite of pouring the Gatorade cooler onto the winning coach. Now this antic was the creative handiwork of Harry Carson, the great Giants linebacker who first poured it on his coach, Bill Parcells, almost twenty years ago. Hey, funny then, very funny, especially since Parcells takes himself so seriously. Ever after, tired, tiresome, predictable. Please spare us.

But I am happy to see football players again. Compared with baseball players, they appear so stylish, with their stockings tucked nicely into their pants at the calf. Football players look smart. They look snappy. But baseball players—almost all of them now wear their pants unbloused, hanging sloppily down to their spikes. They look like the common seamen who fought with Lord Nelson. But there are also a few baseball players who wear their pants too high, almost to the knee. Hey, you're teams, you're supposed to dress alike. Some baseball pants now actually end up higher than basketball shorts. Now who would have ever imagined that? Modern basketball attire is itself both hideous and Darwinian, the survival of the loose fittest.

We're Number 33!

2013

So, we finally have our first official college football championship, and something like fifty million or so fans will be watching to see whether Oregon or Ohio State is the thirty-third-best team in the country. This statement makes me, I admit, both perfectly accurate and infuriatingly facetious.

Certainly, no one would dispute that even the most miserable of the thirty-two NFL teams is far superior to any collegiate squad, but at the same time, a great segment of America will be deeply invested in watching what is, essentially, the equivalent of Triple-A baseball.

It's absolutely intriguing to me—and somehow revealing—that the United States alone places such emphasis on college sport.

Oh, for the record, here and there, other nations possess an abiding interest in some school games. In England, after all, the Oxford-Cambridge crew race has been a fixture since 1829. But we're the odd fellows who've made school football—and later basketball, too—almost as popular as the finest professional leagues.

Now, our sport of football evolved, its prime antecedent being English rugby. But during the latter part of the nineteenth century, as that *other* British game, soccer, began to become popular around the world, our own schoolboys favored the rugby lineage.

Why Americans preferred to run and then throw the ball, rather than kick it, like almost everybody else, remains *the* American mystery, as distinct as our singular American dream. But so it was. And curiously for such a brutal game, it was precisely the fanciest schools—Harvard, Yale, Princeton—that not only advanced the sport but ordained football as a proper social occasion.

As American colleges were often located in out-of-the-way places, a school's football team became something of a marker for that American educational system we were so proud of. In a way, football became the outward and visible sign of the classroom.

Yes, there are great rivalries in our professional sport, but we are a transient society and our deepest loyalties seem to remain more with the colleges we left behind. I've always felt that the emotions we alumni bestow upon our beloved college football teams are more analogous to the passions that citizens in other, smaller countries show their national soccer teams.

The Super Bowl and the World Series are spectaculars, of course, but somehow, even if you don't personally give a hoot about Ohio State or Oregon, the sport carries cultural weight . . . and which team will be the thirty-third-best in the land is a touchstone of America.

Trading Up

2004

I've begun to get the feeling that trades that teams might make are more important in sport than the games that are actually taking place. I've finally decided what explains this. Trades are like showbiz gossip. Trades are like who's going out with whom, who's cheating on whom, who's canoodling with whom. Are Justin Timberlake and Cameron Diaz still together? Will Steve Francis agree to go to Orlando? It's the same silly thing.

As we know, the whole world is now about gossip, so sports needs trade talk to keep up with everyone else. Trades are sexy. It's the same thing: whether or not Brad Pitt and Jennifer Aniston are still happy together or whether or not Ron Artest and Indianapolis are still happy together.

Games are too much like work. They're supposed to be fun, but there isn't a whole lot of mystery to them. Somebody wins and somebody loses, and that's that. What can you say about that on the Internet or talk radio? But speculating on trades is dreamy. Where is Tracy McGrady going? Who will he go for? That's every bit as fascinating as wondering who Britney Spears is going to marry and divorce next week.

It is interesting that you never hear any suggestions that offensive lineman in football should be traded. Only the glamorous backs and the wide receivers. Offensive linemen are like character actors. They don't make the columns, no matter who they go out with. Of course some trades do need extra players to even things up. Some of these are called "future considerations." Some are called "a player to be named later." Some are called "throw-ins." Tell me, could there be anything worse in life than knowing you were a *throw-in*?

Trade talk about the future is so pervasive that it even overwhelms what is actually going on. During the NBA finals, it was hard to care about the games when there were so many hot rumors about where Shaq might be traded to, or where Kobe might go to, or if Rasheed Wallace was going to stay with the Pistons. We aren't satisfied to live in the present anymore in sports. Not even winning is enough anymore.

Drafts, in a way, are even better than trades. Drafts are like Christmas. Everybody gets a present. No wonder everybody likes drafts so much. Drafts are the cosmetic surgery of sports: it's like your team getting tummy tucks or breast enhancements or maybe just a little work around the eyes if you're drafting way down the line.

In football and basketball, there are now experts who do nothing but analyze upcoming drafts all year long. They're exactly like the authorities who do nothing but devote their entire lives to speculating on the status of the Demi Moore–Ashton Kutcher relationship. Then, after the teams pick players, the draft mavens grade the teams on the basis of how much attention the teams paid to their brilliant prognoses. That is very much like the experts who second-guess what the stars wear to the Oscars. How could Uma Thurman ever have picked that mauve gown without a back? How could the Ravens ever have picked an outside linebacker? What was Julia Roberts thinking when she chose the teal lamé with the chiffon sleeves? What were the Nuggets thinking when they took a point guard?

I think we ought to trade Shaq for Catherine Zeta-Jones (with Paris Hilton as a throw-in).

FIVE

Football Are Us

2014

Every election suggests change, so given all the scandals involving football, now's an appropriate time to envision what reforms might be forced upon the sport. Well, I'll tell you: it's tough to mess with football.

Now, to begin with, from hindsight, it was probably misleading to call baseball "the national pastime." The claim was, essentially, based almost entirely on the fact that baseball was the only team sport that boasted a professional presence. The World Series was our World Cup and the Olympics rolled into one.

But really, below that top level, football always ruled our hearts. Unlike sport elsewhere, sport in America grew up as an adjunct to the classroom. Yes, there were the famous three R's—readin', 'ritin, and 'rithmetic—but the fourth R was rivalry. Beating the other school, the other college. In a few areas, most famously Indiana, basketball became the identifying school sport, but almost everywhere else it was football—shown most vividly in Buzz Bissinger's Americana classic, *Friday Night Lights*. Even now, when schools in parts of rural America are forced to consolidate, what the little towns seem to miss most is not their school itself, but their school team.

Forget football's ugly violence. In contrast, it was primarily for sweet reasons that the sport ascended to cultural prominence. Baseball makes a great deal of its association with spring, with the beginning of nature's year, but, much more important, football begins in concert with back-to-school. That's always mattered. Baseball is every day, but football was always on the weekend: an event, parties, dances. Eventually, football even became the centerpiece of homecomings, a touchstone of the fond memory of our youth.

So much is made, and correctly, of baseball's attraction for fathers and sons. But football has an even stronger connection to boys and girls—to, well . . . to sex. Baseball has the seventh-inning stretch; football has halftime—strike up the band and pretty cheerleaders to go with the macho players.

For a burgeoning United States that was flexing its muscles to the world, our manly football was the perfect sport to display the nation's youthful power. Baseball and basketball are about hand-eye coordination, primarily about skill; football—coaches tell boys—is about being a man. Maybe a lot of us need that even more now when, as a nation, we are frustrated. When fathers can't make the living their fathers once did and when men see women in the ascendancy.

That is surely why, for all the evidence now of how football batters male brains, it seems practically invulnerable to change. Football is simply too embedded in our American calendar, in our American culture, and in our American blood—and guts.

The Victim

2003

She ventures how strange it is that it should have happened to her. After all, nothing like it ever happened to anyone else in sports. She remembers the strangeness of it, the sudden pain, or even more, the curiosity. What exactly is going on? And then reflexively she turned, and in the instant before he was subdued, she saw his face just as he began to raise the dagger again. Monica Seles was only nineteen when she was stabbed ten years ago in Hamburg.

Were it not for that terrible, awful, crazy horror, Seles might well have become the greatest female tennis player ever. In the three years leading up to the assault, she had absolutely dominated Steffi Graf, winning eight Grand Slams to her rival's two. That, of course, is why the German lunatic named Guenter Parche stabbed her. He wanted to restore his countrywoman to preeminence. And in point of fact, not only did he succeed, but the German courts took more pity on his insanity than on Seles's suffering. He never served a day behind bars.

Seles, meanwhile, took months to recuperate and also suffered post-traumatic stress syndrome. And in what might have been the cruelest cut of all, her fellow players almost unanimously voted down a proposal to let her keep her number-one ranking. Only Gabriela Sabatini chose humanity over business. "Gaby is a human being," Monica says. "The rest, they treated it like it was a sprained ankle or something."

When Seles finally did come back after twenty-seven months, she was never the same player. Worse, her father, her coach, whom she adored, lingered with cancer for several years before he died in 1998. And yet Seles has stayed in the game, content to be an opponent, a quarterfinalist, a ghost of might-have-been. "But why not?" she asked. She simply loves playing. Tennis is a joy to her, that's all.

I've never met a champion who was less competitive. Her trophies are in the garage, boxed up. Once—imagine this—she told me that her fondest recollections were of exhibitions, because the players were all on their best behavior there. Oh, sure, of course she wants to win, but she does not envision herself jumping the net. "What do you dream of tennis?" I asked her once. Shyly, laughing at herself, she said, "My dream is to be Suzanne Lenglen." She, the glamorous French star of the 1920s—to be like Suzanne, flying through the air, hitting a volley, both feet off the ground, flying.

Seles never complains, never argues, never alibis. Grace attends her. She is a bright shadow of humility amongst foggy egos. There is no one who does not like her a lot. No, she did not need to be almost killed. She did not need to lose her greatness to a madman's knife to become the full, fine person that she is. But we can say that ten years on from hell, Monica Seles has won with a good, brave heart far more than she ever did with a tennis racket. In her own simple words of praise, she's a human being.

Euro Exceptionalism

2015

Wherever you stand on the matter of American exceptionalism, there is one indisputable fact: we *are* the exception when it comes to soccer. For just about every other nation, soccer is *the* sport—a far, far better thing than the American dollar, beer, Google, or sex. Alas, in the United States, soccer has been more commonly identified with soccer moms than soccer players.

But today, soccer is indisputably more visible. Given American football's problems with brain injuries, more of our boys are likely to take up world football. Soccer boosters play up to our growing Hispanic market more frequently than fawning politicians. They pray that young Latino fans will not grow up to be seduced by glamorous gringo games. But . . .

Soccer in America has a curious impediment to its popularity, and the problem is soccer—that is, everybody else's soccer.

After all, Americans believe not only that we are the blessed exception, but that we have the divine right to always have the most exceptional entertainment at our fingertips. The British Empire, theatrical division, seems to have taken up residence here on Broadway. And hey, nobody has any problem with immigration if you're a baseball, basketball, or hockey player.

Except—not exceptionally, but except—in soccer . . . we're a penny stock, we're standby at the airport, we're lawns in Southern California. And all this is happening at a time when Major League Soccer is celebrating its twentieth birthday with some attractive soccer stadiums and a respectable average attendance of nineteen thousand per game.

Except . . . following the MLS is much like taking the Kardashians seriously. What soccer fans really care about is European soccer, and that's quite available on TV. Even our most prominent soccer journalist, Grant Wahl of *Sports Illustrated*, can't think of anything to call ratings for Major League Soccer but "minuscule." English-language ratings remain stagnant. Incredibly, David Beckham, at the height of his deification, could not get Americans to watch American soccer. Even the coach of the American team himself thinks our national players would be better off playing in Europe. Yes, the World Cup attracted terrific interest, but then, so does Kate, the Duchess of Cambridge, every time she has a baby. Then it's back to all the first-rate exceptional diversions that we have right here.

Our fans for football, basketball, baseball, and hockey have fantasy leagues. The fantasy for our soccer fans is that Major League Soccer will somehow become major league, because that's all that exceptional Americans are bred to expect.

I Can Work Longer Than You

2005

Who has the most demanding job in the world? The legendary brain surgeon? The proverbial rocket scientist? The mythical one-armed paperhanger? The president? The pope? No, it is indisputably . . . the football coach. All of them, in college or the pros. How do I know? Just ask them. Football coaches are so tediously self-congratulatory about their devoted work habits.

What a bunch of supercilious braggarts. Do you ever read about any football coach who doesn't work from the dark before dawn to the pitch of night, concentrating, cogitating, nose to the grindstone? No time for friends or family or frivolity if you are a football coach. No sir, all business, 24/7/365, till the cows come home. Football coaches especially love to talk about sleeping in their offices.

Typical is the latest certified genius in the fraternity—Nick Saban, just hired by the Miami Dolphins. What was the absolute first declaration that ushered from Coach Saban's grim lips? That, by golly, all of his assistants should be prepared to eat both lunch and dinner every day at their desks. Time waits for no football coach! Neither does sustenance, hygiene, faith, sex, or merrymaking. Tote that barge, coach, lift that bale.

And really, all football coaches do is watch films. They watch every play at least twenty-two times. Gotta see what every player did every step of the way, every play. Isolate! Rerun! Slo-mo! Then, certain types of plays are put together, computerized, so more late hours can be spent, say, studying all third-down, over-the-middle pass routes on a muddy field in the red zone. No moment is left undigitized. Run it back. Somewhere out there just one other coach may be watching more film than me and my staff.

There used to be an expression that cocaine was God's way of telling us that we have too much money. Well . . .

Football coaches are God's way of telling us that we have too much technology.

Are they any brighter? I doubt it. Why, I know it's true, because I saw in the old movie *Knute Rockne, All American* that Coach Rockne, played by Pat O'Brien, devised a whole new backfield formation on a cocktail napkin in a nightclub watching a line of chorus girls dance and kick. Yes, those were the days when coaches did not need films to think, to be creative. And they had time to go to nightclubs, too.

If only one innovative football coach somewhere would stop pretending that football knowledge is infinite, and tell his assistants to go hog wild: go out to the Olive Garden for a real lunch! Yes! Have a beer! Go home at five and meet your family.

Isn't it revealing that coaches in other sports have no similar work habits? Only football coaches think that the more they work, the more macho they are. My hours are longer than your hours. In fact, when I heard Coach Saban babbling on about no time off for meals, I wanted to call up Wayne Huizenga, the owner of the Dolphins, who had just hired Saban, and tell him what the late philosopher–basketball coach Al McGuire once observed.

What Coach McGuire said was, "Anybody who can't get his job done in thirty-five hours a week is obviously unqualified for the job."

The Snakes in the Garden of Sports

2015

Sports may be dismissed as inconsequential child's play, but there is, in counterpoint, the ideal that sport is our best model for human fairness and equality—a Garden of Eden with competition. But, of course, there are snakes in this athletic garden. Rules will be broken. To my mind there are, in ascending order, three kinds of transgressions. The first is the most simple: transgressions committed in the heat of the action, instinctively, because of frustration, failure, or anger. There are referees to tend to that misconduct.

The second type of violation falls more into the realm of regulation. For example, who is eligible to play? There are age restrictions in youth sport and academic requirements in college. Also, as with any civil enterprise, sport can deny entrance to the garden to anyone who misbehaves in the public sphere. For instance: *Thou shalt not batter women or children.* Alas, that is famously more honored in the breach. Most sports also publish specific ordinances that participants must observe. It was here, for best example, that Pete Rose came a cropper.

Ah, but then, finally, foremost, there are violations against the very nature of the game—these are, invariably, premeditated.

In any sport, once the lines are drawn, what we have on the field are, in toto, athletes and the proper equipment. That's it. In religious terms, these are the priests and the relics, and to deface or distort either is not just an infraction, but a contamination. That's why athletes who take performance-enhancing drugs are, to continue the analogy, sacrilegious.

And no less, those who would maliciously alter the equipment. In hindsight, all of us made a terrible mistake in looking upon someone like Gaylord Perry—he, the pitcher infamous for loading up his deliveries with what we quaintly call "foreign substances"—as a sort of sassy, picaresque figure, who was merely tilting at the windmills of authority. Nonsense. Perry and his ilk didn't abuse baseballs; they abused *baseball*. Do not let that happen again.

Therefore, likewise, even if it was no more than an illegal *whiff* of air that was willfully, with foresight, removed from the New England Patriots' footballs—with Tom Brady's direction or mere acquiescence—Brady is guilty of purposely defiling the very artifacts that make the game fair and square. It is not enough to say that everybody cheats a little, or that, gee, there wasn't all that much difference in the balls, or that people are picking on the poor Patriots.

Games are played by natural flesh-and-blood people using authorized equipment. If either is illegally distorted, it's not just a crime against the game but a wound to the whole essence of sport.

Chicago

1996

I could not help but notice that Cardinal Bernadine of Chicago died last Thursday just hours before a revival of the musical *Chicago* opened on Broadway.

Of course, there is no equating the two links of this coincidence. The cardinal was not only this unbelievably good person, but this force for good—somehow able, in this adversarial world, to bring us together with grace and civility. And *Chicago*, the musical, is only a play. What constructs the paradox, though, is that it succeeds wonderfully, darkly, by celebrating all those things that the cardinal was not—hypocritical, cynical, venal.

Naturally, any metropolis is a creature of extremes, but never, it seemed to me, has anything been writ so contradictorily, so starkly, so perfectly about this one place—Chicago.

Chicago—the city of Michael Jordan and Oprah Winfrey.

I think Chicago is the one town that best stands for the United States. It calls itself the second city, but, really, New York is more of the world than just of this country, and Los Angeles is only marginally a city—just people and cars and images all living uneasily together in motion. Chicago is us.

Us—extremes! Hey, Chicago is the city of the greatest losers in the nation. The Cubbies!

But Chicago also offers the most obvious representation of the sport of football—Da Bears! They from Sandburg's "city of big shoulders . . . stormy, husky, brawling . . ." Da Bears!

Maybe Chicago is so much more American because all the swells and dandies really do fly over it, going coast to coast, or deign only to meet briefly at the O'Hare Hilton and then be gone.

Could Siskel and Ebert have worked in New York or L.A.? No way. Neither could have Northwestern . . . or Mike Royko . . . or Ernie Banks . . . or Harry Caray.

But Chicago was *due* Michael Jordan. It was serendipity.

As the one most extraordinary American athletic figure of the first half century, Babe Ruth was somehow meant to end up in our apex—New York. So, it seems, was the one most extraordinary American athletic figure of the second half of the century properly destined for our model, for Chicago.

Always before, things in sport started in Chicago and then moved on. So much of modern baseball was formed in that cauldron. Even sportswriting as we know it developed best with Chicago baseball. The Cubs and the White Sox ruled the national pastime when the Yankees were something still called the Highlanders. But after the Black Sox scandal, the diamond power flowed out of the Windy City.

Likewise, the glamour of pro football in the beginning centered on Chicago—Papa George Halas and the Monsters of the Midway. But when the NFL became fashionable, it left the Bears behind, bruisers of another time.

And basketball. The Harlem Globetrotters might've had a New York name, but they were a Chicago team—most famous in all the world. Only when pro basketball became legit, the

Chicago Gears, the Chicago Stags, and the Chicago Zephyrs all failed.

Aha, but at last when pro basketball became stylish then came the Bulls and Mr. Jordan. The worm finally turned. And now Chicago is on Broadway and in heaven and in all the standings. More than ever, it's our American city.

Put an End to It

2011

Hear ye, hear ye: the court of public opinion will now come to order in the class-action suit by disturbed football fans against dopey football players who act like imbeciles in the end zone after scoring a touchdown.

Your honor, the plaintiffs call to the stand a man of great taste, good manners, and exquisite judgment—namely, me.

What is this?

Why is football the only sport where every score—and most mere tackles behind the line of scrimmage—will now produce extravagant dramatic exertions that we haven't seen since silent movies went out? And it's only getting worse. Mary Pickford is rolling over in her grave. Not to mention the 360s that Vince Lombardi is doing.

For comparison's sake, think about how other athletes celebrate achievement. In baseball, just a bashful tip o' the cap. Fans who catch foul balls carry on more than actual players who hit home runs. In hockey, teammates wearing gloves rub the helmet of the guy who scored the goal. It's very sanitary, hockey exultation is.

The most memorable emotional outburst in basketball was simply a midcourt shrug that Michael Jordan offered after an especially spectacular display. Golfers momentarily raise their club in modest salute after sinking a long putt. Tennis players can't even bring themselves to smile.

True story: I am sitting in Charles Barkley's house with him, watching Pete Sampras win a tiebreaker with one extraordinary shot after another. Sampras just lowers his head each time. Barkley is screaming at the television set—literally screaming: "Come on, Pete, come on. Stop playing with your strings. At least look up. Please, please."

But football is different. Football players prance and preen, and stomp and strut, and even put on extended little mime routines like Marcel Marceau on a real bad day.

It's terribly puerile. It drives the purists crazy. We've gone from three yards and a cloud of dust to chorus boys in the end zone. In football! In the manly game! There's no dancing in football! . . . Five-six-seven-eight.

But, hey, purists, get over it. Because it doesn't seem to bother the opponents—the very ones being ridiculed. They just wait for their own turn to act like clowns. Doesn't seem to bother the coaches. They never seem to fine the players who get penalties for "excessive" celebrating, whatever "excessive" has come to mean. Doesn't seem to bother the announcers. They never criticize the goofballs. Doesn't seem to bother most of the fans.

By now, in fact, rude end-zone choreography is just part of the game, like busty cheerleaders and concussions and tailgating.

The court thereby rules that all football players who act like creeps in the end zone are guilty—but out on appeal, because the truth is, to most fans, that childish showing-off is . . . appealing.

An update:

Because most touchdowns are scored by African Americans, and so most of the end-zone high jinks are therefore, ipso facto, performed by black players, I was accused of being a racist for this commentary. NPR felt obliged to conduct a lengthy review, examining other of my past commentaries that touched, no matter how tangentially, on race, to see if there was a pattern of prejudice. I was interviewed at length by the NPR ombudsman, and while it was a polite inquiry it was clear that I had some explaining to do. I remember pointing out, during the interrogation that, just as I did not like the way football players, who largely happen to be African American, carry on in the end zone, I was no fan of kabuki, but that a layman's critical opinion about one small part of that culture did not make me anti-Japanese. Taste does not translate into bias, although it often seems to be taken for that nowadays.

As it was, I was completely exonerated of the charge of racism, and even received a full apology, which I appreciated, but the larger point is how sensitive the topic of race in sports is. I will admit that I am on tenterhooks every time I write any commentary that merely verges on the subject of race. I know that every word will be parsed; the nuance police are on full alert where race is involved in sports journalism (or, I suppose, in every kind of journalism), and this situation results in either an evasion of the subject or some embarrassing pussyfooting, which I don't think serves either black or white people—or sports— well in the long run.

SIX

Give and Go

2013

Basketball offers its fans the ultimate contradiction. On the one hand, it's the sport that most depends on its stars. On the other, it's the most intimate—even organic—of all the team games, with its players more fundamentally involved with one another. Both of these opposing realities are rooted in the same base.

After all, among team sports, basketball has the fewest players—five—and usually only a couple of additional substitutes play substantial amounts of time. Short or tall or whatever position, basketball players all must handle the ball, play both offense and defense, and work together. *Switch* is the revealing basketball word. At least for a while, you must become me, and me you.

By contrast, football teams are a sum of many completely alien specialties; baseball hitters and pitchers are different creatures. Hockey and soccer both have goalies altogether separate from their teammates, and they're likewise divided by field geography or wholesale substitutions.

Ah, but a basketball team is a nest.

Yet precisely because there are so few players, and they're close to the spectators, skimpily attired, unmasked, uncapped, basketball players are so visible. It's easier to connect with them.

More hoop heroes are known just by their first names, like the regulars in the tabloids.

This is as true now, with Kobe and Melo, as it was with Wilt and Elgin way back then. Fans pay to go see the stars and are disappointed when they don't perform spectacularly.

But then, inevitably, the same hoop cognoscenti rhapsodize about how these heroes can't do it alone—they can't even be selfish!—and it is *really* the intricately integrated team play that we *true* basketball fans come to see.

It is a harmless deceit, but a universal hoop hypocrisy.

Never, perhaps, has this conflict been more evident than now, in the NBA finals, where the sainted brotherhood of basketball purity, otherwise known as the San Antonio Spurs, are playing the LeBron Heat.

The Spurs, of course, also possess a wonderful player, but he is the rare spotlight-aversive star, who is simply known as Tim Duncan—which is, in fact, his square name. With Tim Duncan, little out-of-the-way San Antonio has won four championships, so everybody effusively praises the Spurs' legendary teamwork while simultaneously criticizing shallow fans—not me, of course—but all those other philistines, who are blinded by individual showoffs. Whoever shall win the championship this year, the paradox in the sport will never subside. It is a game of wonderfully fluid interaction among a handful of players— no sport has ever been celebrated better than by its signature phrase: give and go—but in basketball, as in life, we may dutifully celebrate the aggregate, but we're always spellbound by the exceptional. We swear by the Spurs; we are mesmerized by LeBron.

Pretty Good

2003

Well, somebody has to do it. Somebody has to stand up for the oppressed, and so it is I who come now to the defense of Anna Kournikova. Good heavens, there is no end to the amount of sneering censure that she endures. Among celebrities, only Madonna receives more criticism, and she asks for it, right? It's almost as if Kournikova has made it a crime to be pretty—and remember, before Anna suffered some serious injuries she was a really terrific young player, top ten. But all her jealous critics ever do is remind us that Anna's never won a tournament. It's like part of her name. Anna Kournikova, who's never won a tournament, brushed her teeth this morning.

Hey, I know it's not fair that women's looks matter more than men's. But where Kournikova, who's never won a tournament, is penalized is with this ridiculous assumption that somehow sports is different from the rest of the world. Terrible actresses get good parts because they're prettier than better actresses. Dreadful singers have hit songs because their figures are better than their voices. Nobody raises a stink. But along comes Kournikova, who's never won a tournament—not to mention this bevy of other good-looking, young female tennis players—and a lot of women (and some men, too) get positively vicious because male spectators want to watch her.

Hey, may we get real? The way it is, males enjoy watching pretty girls doing . . . anything . . . walking, standing still, sitting . . . at work, at school, at church—yes, even there—so why should we think anything would be different with men and boys in the sports world? But the equality police get all out of sorts when fans linger longer over blondes than backhands. And it's not as if Kournikova, who's never won a tournament, hurts her sport. Billie Jean King said long ago that if men come out to ogle pulchritude in sneakers, they may stay around long enough to eventually like the tennis.

Given that athletics features bodies, for goodness' sake, it's a little much to expect fans not to notice physical appearance. It ain't just the babes, after all. During this year's U.S. Open, the tabloids have been full of hunks—sultry photos of a shirtless Andy Roddick, a smoldering Robby Ginepri—with breathless talk of their showbiz romances. And, sure, Tiger Woods is a pretty good golfer, but let's be honest: especially compared with his rivals on the golf tour, it doesn't hurt his image that he is one cute guy. If you were trying to make a pinup calendar for the PGA, you couldn't get past April.

The argument against admiring beauty in sports is based on the premise that because sports are determined by merit, so, too, should popularity be. But other extraneous personal factors have always trumped simple success. We want to know more about the meanest players, and the smartest and the tallest and the shortest, and the mouthiest and the weirdest. Nobody was disturbed when nutsy Dennis Rodman got more publicity than far better players. Relax, self-appointed arbiters of athletic taste. Relax and admire good-looking athletes, female and male, for being pretty and for playing pretty, both. And Anna, who's never won a tournament, just keep on doing what you do . . . whatever that may be.

Mister Misses

2010

At a time when newspaper sports departments are disappearing as fast as Baltimore Orioles fans, I'm delighted to have the *Wall Street Journal* aboard as a new member of what has long been characterized as the toy department. Yes, America's sobersided business gazette has started a ballyhooed section in the New York market that features local news, culture, and . . . sports.

However, while I admit that I'm not qualified to advise the *Journal* on how to write about credit default swaps, may I be so impudent as to dare tell the *Journal* that if it purports to cover sports on its gray pages, it must get on the same page with the rest of us "World's Jock Glitterati."

That is, my dear stock market friends: if you're going to write about games, you don't call players "Mr." or "Ms." In sports sections, or on sports TV, or on sports Internet the world over, nobody—not even fancy-pants team owners—gets to be a Mr. or Mrs. Or a Señor or a Herr or a Mademoiselle. Why, they don't even use courtesy titles on the jolly old Wimbledon scoreboard anymore.

But because it is the *Journal's* style to refer to hedge funders in their bespoke suits and Turnbull & Asser shirts and ties by their courtesy title, it has foolishly decided to maintain this same policy in sports. Thus we have a discussion of a "Mr. Braden's perfect game," a "Mr. Barajas behind the plate," and a "Mr. James, who works for a Cleveland firm." Having the *Journal* cover sports is rather like having Miss Jane Austen write them for you, with Mr. Darcy batting and Mr. Bingley pitching.

Thank heavens the legendary Mr. Grantland Rice was not working for Mr. Rupert Murdoch when he wrote about a Notre Dame backfield—that most famous line ever to appear on a sports page—or it would've come out this way: "Outlined against a blue-gray October sky, the Four Horsemen rode again. In dramatic lore they were known as Famine, Pestilence, Destruction, and Death. These are only aliases. Their real names are Mr. Struhldreher, Mr. Miller, Mr. Crowley, and Mr. Layden."

Or as Howard Cosell would've called out memorably on *Journal* television: "Down goes Mr. Frazier! Down goes Mr. Frazier!"

Now, it is true that there was a double standard on the sports pages for many years. Whereas male athletes would be identified by only their last name, it was felt that sportswomen could not be treated so rudely. Thus we had "Laver vs. Rosewall" . . . but "Mrs. King vs. Miss Bueno."

If anything, though, now we are heading downscale, where more and more athletes—both genders, all sports—are referred to in the media simply by their first name or a nickname. Thus we have Kobe and A-Rod and Serena and T.O.—all far better known that way, informally, than by what appears on their passports.

Yes, *Wall Street Journal*, we welcome you to the arena, but please: one of the nice things about *our* business is that there are no misters in sport. Just players.

An update:
Not long after I delivered this commentary, the Journal *changed its policy and dropped the titles in its sports pages.*

His Refuge

2004

You're Kobe Bryant, and wherever you go people are staring at you. You're up for sexual assault—charged with raping a young woman. You are a so-called little man in basketball, a guard, but, in fact, you are six feet seven, and so you can't put on sunglasses and a hat like some little movie star and get lost in the crowd.

You are Kobe Bryant, and people shout at you. Or they whisper behind your back. One or the other. Some of them hold up signs at you. The paparazzi dog you. You just look straight ahead and pretend not to notice. Almost everybody has an opinion about you. Nobody except, of course, you and the woman knows for sure what happened in that hotel room in Colorado last summer, but most people have made up their minds. You are an ogre, a monster. Or you are a victim.

You have bodyguards and you fly on chartered jets or you are ferried about in limousines. But sooner or later you surface, because you are still a basketball player, and you go out on the court in the spotlight and play another game. Usually beautifully. How do you do it, Kobe?

Through the years a lot of athletes with trouble in their lives have been able to use the arena as a refuge. Out there, on the court, on the field, they could forget everything that is swirling about them and just lose themselves doing what they do best, playing a game.

But you are Kobe Bryant, and however good you are, the court is another quagmire. Your teammates don't particularly like you. Anyway, at the best, they don't understand you. They need you, but they're jealous of you, too. Don't shoot so much, Kobe. No, tonight, shoot, Kobe, save us.

You're a different breed of cat. You grew up in Italy, an American abroad—an African American abroad. You came back home but you really didn't know how to fit in—not even with your teammates. It's no different on the Lakers from what it was in Lower Merion Township, Pennsylvania.

You skipped college. Maybe you could have made friends there. A fresh start. But you went right to the pros, so young, so by yourself. You're always alone. Who do you turn to, Kobe Bryant?

You go home to your wife. What do you two talk about? Does she believe you . . . that you didn't rape that woman? Anyway, she knows you cheated on her. Sure, professional athletes are advertised as tomcats, but you weren't supposed to be like that. Then your wife found out that this wasn't so. However it was with her, now it must be different. You married her when you were both so young. Your father didn't want you to. She wasn't a black woman. That broke up the family. One more tie undone.

Even if you don't go to jail, life always seems to get narrower and tighter for you. And now it's the playoffs, and you're supposed to do even more, but all the time knowing that in just a few months, a few weeks, you could be adjudged guilty, sent away for years, maybe decades, never to play a game of basketball again. And the people keep staring at you, shouting, whispering.

You're Kobe Bryant accused, indicted. Shoot, Kobe. Pass, Kobe. Star, Kobe. How in the world do you wake up every day and do it? How?

You're It Is Out

2006

In the growing American realm of no child shall be left behind in this real world, comes word that more schools have
banned—if you can believe this—tag. Yes! School districts as diverse as Cheyenne, Wyoming; Spokane, Washington; Charles-
ton, South Carolina; Santa Monica, California; and Attleboro,
Massachusetts have decreed that the game children have been
playing, well, forever and ever and ever is too dangerous to
either the physical health or the mental well-being of our little
twenty-first-century darlings.

This, of course, comes on the heels of the attempts to ban
dodgeball, another movement which has enjoyed great success
in taking the spontaneous fun out of growing up. But tag? Ban
tag? What's next? Not letting kids sell lemonade because they
don't have commercial licenses? In the immortal words of an
elementary school principal in Attleboro: recess is a time when
accidents can happen.

What a revelation! Why, a little boy or girl might actually
even scruff a knee or scrape an elbow. But a professor at Eastern
Connecticut State University finds tag so baleful an experience
that he has placed it in the physical education hall of shame.

All this at a time when we have an absolute epidemic of
childhood obesity in this country. But for goodness' sake, don't

let kids play games at recess. They might bump into each other. They also might burn up a few calories. Would you rather have your child running around or sitting on his fat rear end playing video games?

But for the pompous protectors of our youth, it's not just that somebody playing tag may have to put a Band-Aid on. No, it's a debilitating emotional experience as well. Educators refer to tag as an elimination game, which means it can be upsetting if you get put out.

The trouble is that the kids who are the slowest and the least athletic are likely to be losers. Duh! Nobody's good at everything. All life is a pecking order, and you might as well find out where it is that you peck.

In music class, I was the one who was only allowed to play the triangle because I was so unrhythmic. Hey, I sucked it up and got on with it.

I hate to say it, but that's the way it works in every phase of life. Please, I'm not trying to be Darwinian, but sparing children from their deficiencies is delusional. There are a lot of us who think that kids would be a lot better off if adults would just butt out and let children be children and play children's games. I'll bet you this, too. I'll bet you the spoilsports who are trying to eliminate tag were the ones who were themselves always *it* at recess.

I'm Frank Deford, and I approve this message, because somebody has to call the grown-ups who ban tag enemies of childhood.

The Last in the Line

2012

Now that Joe Paterno has been relieved from his job in Happy Valley, we must ponder whether we will ever see his like again. But please: I am now, you understand, talking about *Coach* Paterno. Let us, for the moment, put aside how the citizen whose credo was "Success with Honor" acted with regard to pedophilia: so without sensitivity, so irresponsibly, so—ultimately—cold-bloodedly. That will sully Paterno's memory forever.

But, simply, for now: Joe Paterno, the coach, which is what he still was—it's hard to recall this now—barely eleven weeks ago. Will, in fact, any college coach ever again possess the power he did over his university?

Well, almost surely not. Paterno's long tenure at an insulated campus, combined with how venerable he became and how upright he was supposed to be in conducting his program, is a circumstance unlikely to be duplicated.

On the other hand, to suggest that someone like Nick Saban at Alabama or Urban Meyer, who just took over at Ohio State, does not possess authority far beyond contractual niceties is naive. Big-time football coaches are the Cardinal Richelieu among state university royalty—or the Rasputin, if you are of a more cynical bent.

But in the matter of time in grade, Paterno's career will probably never be replicated. Unlike, say, basketball coaches, who are operating in a smaller, more personal universe, football is so much more hierarchical. You have to work your way up: assistant; coordinator; head coach mid-major; head coach big-time. It takes a while. Paterno himself was almost forty before he got his chance.

His closest basketball peers—like Mike Krzyzewski at Duke, Jim Boeheim at Syracuse, or Dean Smith and Bobby Knight, retired, all made Division-I head coach at an age when football coaches are still climbing the ladder. Moreover, because basketball is more intimate, a coach can better create his own comfortable nest. Besides, because so much more money is involved, there is more pressure on football coaches and less forgiveness for the losers; the best coaches today are constantly being lured to other colleges by big-money boosters.

As for pro sports, longevity is even more problematic because the players don't turn over every four years, and the veterans stop listening to most coaches after a while. Even a capable coach moves on. Of coaches in the four major professional team sports, Gregg Popovich of the NBA's San Antonio Spurs has lasted the longest: fifteen years. At Penn State, after fifteen, Paterno still had thirty-one more years to go.

So, no: when Paterno was fired in November, it concluded a career that we can surely never even imagine again. In the time he reigned, though, more and more celebrity, veneration, and prerogative accrued to college football coaches, and notwithstanding what he did not do in the matter of coach Jerry Sandusky, Joe Paterno had much to do with giving other coaches a sovereignty they never previously possessed.

Hailing Proudly
Too Often

2006

Watching the World Cup, I find it especially moving at the start of each game when the two teams stand as the national anthems of their countries are played. I'm particularly touched by the teams who stand for their anthem with their arms about one another's shoulders.

And it must be absolutely chilling for the players and people of some small nation like Ghana or Paraguay to hear its anthem played in tandem with that of England or Italy or the United States.

Playing the anthems seems so right here. After all, the World Cup is a very special competition between the nations of the world that is contested only every four years.

Okay, but then tune into some everyday hockey game between, say, Calgary and Nashville or some baseball game between Toronto and Texas. Every time, it's obligatory to start off by playing the national anthems of both the United States and Canada.

Come on! Countries aren't playing in games like this, just municipalities which have paid professionals to represent their franchises. We might as well also play the national anthems of, say, the Czechs and the Swedes or the Dominicans and Venezuelans who might incidentally be hired hands on these metropolitan rosters.

What is it with this nationalism—even, I would say, forced patriotism—that only inflicts national anthems upon sports in this country? Hey, they're just amusements. In New York, you go to Madison Square Garden, to Shea Stadium, to Yankee Stadium, for a game, the performance begins with "The Star-Spangled Banner." You go to Carnegie Hall for a concert, Lincoln Center for a ballet, Broadway for a play, all you hear before the show starts is a warning to turn off your cell phones. Why is there a difference?

In fact, the playing of an anthem has long become such a rote experience in American sports that it was years ago when I first heard what was already an old joke then. What are the last two words of the national anthem?

"Play ball!"

The anthem has become so everyday at sports events here that some years ago it even became necessary for public-address announcers to explain why exactly it is that we are playing the song: "To honor America, will you please rise?"

We have to be told the reason to stand up?

But, you see, in the United States, the anthem has been reduced to just another gimmick like the seventh-inning stretch.

In fact, "The Star-Spangled Banner" is so ordinary now that at championship events like the Super Bowl, when the anthem would be a nice, appropriate gesture, it's not enough just to sing our country's song. No, it's so run-of-the-mill that now we also have to then have a bunch of fighter jets fly over. The national anthem has become a lounge act for military showbiz.

Next Tuesday is our American national holiday, the Fourth of July. Wouldn't it be nice if all baseball teams would agree to swear off playing the anthem at every game during the season and only play it once a year, on our Independence Day?

That would be enough. Look out to center field. Just as Francis Scott Key assured us, our flag is still there.

SEVEN

Kept Men

2008

Some things in sport, like some things in life, never really get changed, even when they are indefensible. We say: "Life is unfair," and move on. Sports, though, are supposed to be altogether fair. Ah, the level playing field! But, alas, that's only so when referees are around.

Still, every now and then, it's worth bringing up some glaring inequity, even if it's pointless to do so.

So now—when college basketball is in full swing and college football is at its climax, with bowls jammed with high-paying customers, with television revenue pouring in, not to mention all the money that hotels and airlines and restaurants and souvenir salesmen and announcers and sportswriters and coaches and athletic directors are raking in—is a good time to lament anew that, my gracious, isn't it interesting that the only people not making money are the people actually playing the games.

Yes, it is perfectly unconscionable that big-time college football and basketball players go unpaid. They are employees, and deserve to be paid based on the National Labor Relations Act.

First of all, a little history is in order. When college football became a popular sensation more than a hundred years ago, the concept of amateurism was in full sway. Okay. All Olympic athletes, for example, had to live by what was always called "the amateur ideal."

But all that has changed. The most popular Olympic sports have all gone pro. Today, in all the world, among big-ticket spectator sports, virtually the only athletes who are not paid are our college football and basketball players—whose numbers include so many poor African Americans.

That this should be so in the United States, bastion of both freedom and capitalism, makes it even worse. That this should remain the case when college sports charge Broadway ticket prices and pay their coaches literally millions of dollars makes it even more shameful.

Moreover, colleges always emphasize that football and basketball make so much money that they pay for the entire athletic program. To me, this only adds to the cynicism. Not only do poor black kids get no remuneration for their work; they are expected to carry all these other coaches and players and teams on their backs with their unpaid labor.

Basically, a scholarship boils down to a device to keep the players on the premises where they can perform their services for free. Okay, they get a lot of perks. They live well. They're the equivalent of what we used to call "kept women."

Besides, why is it that only athletes must perform for the so-called love of the game? Nobody cares if college kids who are actors or musicians or writers or dancers can make a buck using their talent. Why is an athlete any different?

But, at the end of the day, it isn't an economic issue so much as a moral one. It's absolutely evil that only here in the United States do we allow this unscrupulous nineteenth-century arrangement to continue to exist—and nobody anymore hardly even bothers to bring up this awful injustice.

Seashells
and Balloons

2001

What the world saw of Al McGuire was some wisecracking character from a Sean O'Casey play, a charming sharpie. What this disguised, however, was a shrewd and very calculating businessman who lived much more prudently than he ever let on.

He grew up tending bar in his father's New York saloon, scuffling on the streets and the basketball courts, and he didn't look back on that life as romantic at all. His office was decorated with images of sad clowns. Boy, did Al know irony and contradiction. Flashy as he was, his true self was revealed in his teams at Marquette, which won year after year with a cool dispassionate defense, with control.

McGuire lived happily amid his many friends, doing as much as possible of what he called "going barefoot in the wet grass," which fit with another favorite phrase of his, "congratulating the temporary," that is, live for the moment.

But at the same time, McGuire, born an immigrant's son, framed by the Depression he grew up in, always had to, as he said, "squirrel some nuts away." "Frank," he told me, "never undress until you die, Frank." That meant simply be sure you have something to leave behind. I asked him if at the end, if there would be more than what his wife, Pat, and his kids needed, what should they do with the rest? Al thought for a moment. "Build a park for poor people," he said.

And yes, that would be a very appropriate way to remember Alfred Emanuel McGuire, who died the other day, at the age of seventy-two. He hated to go. Life for him was what he called "seashells and balloons." But I'm sure he didn't complain. One day out of the blue, he just blurted out to me, "Frank, what a great life I've had, Frank." McGuire, you see, was not good with names, even his own players'. But when he did know your name, he would use it twice, like bookends.

And then always he said so many wry, vivid things, like "Every obnoxious fan has a wife at home who dominates him." And "Blacks will have arrived only when we start seeing black receptionists who aren't good-looking." And "If a guy comes home with flowers and says they're not for anything, they're for something." And "Dealing with problems, with differences, that's coaching. Running patterns is not coaching."

In fact, he was sort of the anti-coach. He hated films and x's and o's and off-court discipline. Coaching, he said, was a mistress. He specifically hired what he called "complementary assistants," men very different from what he was, "first communion guys" who he needed to do the everyday coaching stuff. Al himself was out front. "Frank, only one of us can wear the brassiere, Frank," he explained. More than anybody I ever knew, Al McGuire simply got it.

I'm sure, for example, that when he gave up coaching in 1977, still in his forties, at the height of his powers, he knew he would be a huge success as a TV analyst, and he was. But, oh, how he went out, winning the NCAA championship with his last game. Al adored country and western lyrics. After he won the title, I sent him a telegram with one of my favorites that I thought was apropos: "The girls get prettier at closing time." He loved that.

And now that the absolute last round has been served in Al McGuire's wonderful life, let me only add: Al, what a great life you gave us, Al.

Keeping the
Elephants Away

2003

Unfortunately when you watch the Super Bowl this Sunday, you will not be allowed to see a commercial touting the elegant vacation properties of Las Vegas. The National Football League has vetoed it because even though the commercial doesn't even mention gambling, the NFL, whose popularity is bulwarked by gambling, wants to pretend that it will have nothing to do with gambling. The decision is not hypocritical so much as it is simply childish. Really, it's time for the NFL and major-league baseball, the National Basketball Association, and the National Hockey League to all grow up and treat gambling maturely.

Please, let's face it, where there are games, people will bet. It's idiotic to run away from that fact. Indeed, in many countries, national lotteries are based on soccer results. In a grown-up place like England, you can walk into any neighborhood betting shop and get a wager down on just about any event, including even, say, the British Open and Wimbledon. And, you know, I haven't heard a single suggestion that Phil Mickelson and Anna Kournikova haven't won the championships because gamblers have gotten to them.

But the American sports leagues love to maintain this fiction that gamblers are a threat to their games. By making a big fuss about this, the leagues can then shout about what a wonderful job they're doing in saving their games from fixes. It's like the guy sitting on the street corner waving his arms. "What are you doing?" "I'm keeping the elephants away." "I don't see any elephants." "See, I'm keeping them away."

The NFL, the NHL, the NBA, and baseball are doing a great job of keeping the elephants away. The last time there was any real evidence of even an attempted fix in major team sports was half a century away in the NBA with a rogue player named Jack Molinas. The last time there was an attempted fix in the NFL was 1946. It has been more than eighty years since gamblers seriously tried to fix baseball games. The players in our professional leagues simply make too much money, which is why what few attempted fixes there are invariably involve poor college kids with no pro future. Yet the leagues have a whipping boy. It would be as if President Bush regularly talked about the threat to America of the Bolsheviks or the Barbary pirates.

The NFL denies the existence of Las Vegas. The NBA wouldn't place a franchise in Toronto until pro basketball was banned from legal sports books in Ontario, and baseball waves Pete Rose like a bloody shirt. Rose mostly speaks nonsense, but the one place where he makes perfect sense is in pointing out what a double standard he is punished under. Drug offenders in baseball and other sports get all sorts of second chances. Drugs, not gambling, threaten the integrity of all sports, but it's easier to scream about the imaginary dangers of gambling fixes than to deal with the real drug problem.

And if the NFL wanted to be honestly concerned, the commercials it would ban from its games would be food advertisements. More and more of its players are grotesque three-hundred-pounders, walking coronaries who are fattened up for games like geese for the liver pâté. Hey, Commissioner Tagliabue, Vegas ain't the problem. Heal thyself. But since NPR believes in fair play, may I say to all Americans: Go to Las Vegas, that Xanadu in the desert. Enjoy its many splendors and be sure to go to a friendly sports book and bet on the Super Bowl. And however you bet, you can be absolutely assured of an honest game. All the Bucs and all the Raiders will be playing their hardest.

Real vs. Reality

2004

May I make the simple suggestion that a prime reason why national television ratings for sports may have declined so is because of reality television shows.

It would seem to me that reality TV is nothing more than a form of sport. It's a competition, a game, but on a coast-to-coast basis it's more emotionally appealing than many of our sports, so I have to believe that as many people get more interested in the reality shows, they lose some interest in old-fashioned sports.

The constant problem that sports in this country suffer from is that there are just too many teams playing too many games. People—especially local fans—can follow their teams, but only the hard-core zealots monitor a whole sport. As a consequence, especially in the team sports with myriad games—baseball, basketball, and hockey—home attendance may remain high, while at the same time ratings for national games decrease. That may sound contradictory, but it makes sense.

Let's take just one city as an example. The good people in Dallas may have cared passionately about their basketball and hockey teams, but as soon as the Stars and Mavericks were eliminated in the playoffs, I would suspect that a goodly number of the Dallas fans dropped their interest altogether in the NBA and NHL playoffs and started devoting their attention to the local baseball team, the Texas Rangers.

Reality TV focuses. There are only a small number of competitors and we get to meet them and know them well—a whole lot better than our friends in Dallas ever get to know the Calgary Flames or the Milwaukee Bucks during the regular season. In many respects, in fact, reality TV shows essentially start with the elimination playoffs—which concentrate the mind—without having to bother us with the long, boring regular season.

Reality television shows also are scheduled for just once a week. Every competition becomes important—in TV language, appointment viewing. Football has become the one traditional team sport that continues to have a growing national audience, and a large reason for this is that there are only a limited number of games, with the vast majority taking place on the weekends. It's no coincidence, I don't think, that the one sport which has shown great ratings gains in the past few years is NASCAR, which follows the once-a-weekend NFL model. This year, NASCAR has even dramatically whipped the NBA and the NHL in national TV ratings.

NASCAR is like an all-star reality show every week. Everybody who follows the sport knows all the major drivers. Contrast NASCAR to the PGA, where each week there are different contenders. The casual fan can't keep them all straight, so he only stays tuned when Tiger Woods has a chance. Familiarity is so important when we are watching any kind of game. If we know the contestants, we can decide whether we want to root for or against them. That's why the NFL and NBA drafts are more interesting to more people than most actual games. We become familiar with the prospects before the draft and get involved.

Anyway, with all the competition from the new once-a-week television contests, maybe major-league baseball, the NBA, and the NHL are just going to have to settle for having intense local followings with declining national impact. And the hero that a nation turns its lonely eyes to is not going to be a great star who hits home runs or scores baskets but some guy who sings songs or picks a bride or gets a job with Donald Trump.

Yes, indeed: your new American idol. That's reality.

That Sunday of Ours

2004

Is the Super Bowl important? I don't mean to the NFL or to the Panthers or Patriots or to the people who hold big bets. I mean: has it become an important slice of America? It is, after all, just so big.

We have, for example, reports of water pressure being threatened here and there because almost everybody in the United States suddenly flushes at the same time, during time-outs. More pizza is delivered on Super Bowl Sunday than on any other day of the year. Almost as many Americans watch the Super Bowl as bother to vote for president.

As a matter of fact, not once in the last decade have Americans watched any show in greater numbers than a Super Bowl. In that sense, the Super Bowl is really retro; it takes us back to another era, when Americans had few choices on television—or radio before that—when so many of us all made sure to gather round with each other to hear *Amos and Andy* or watch *I Love Lucy* or *Laugh-In* or *The Ed Sullivan Show* or the *Miss America* pageant.

Yet unlike all those shows with mass popular appeal, the Super Bowl offers little emotional contact for most of its viewers. And it absolutely flies in the face of our celebrity worship.

Whereas baseball, basketball, and hockey can only count on larger audiences for their championships if the most popular teams or the biggest stars are on display, none of that matters for the Super Bowl.

Really, how many millions of people who will camp before the TV this Sunday could name a single Carolina Panther? Or which Carolina it is, exactly, or what city in wherever?

I think one of the reasons that the commercials for the Super Bowl attract so much attention is that, invariably, we are much more familiar with the products than the teams, which incidentally play the game. Pepsi and Budweiser are in our consciousness far more than the Pats and the Cats.

Likewise, Willie Nelson, who will be hawking the services of H&R Block, is much better known than any of the players.

Yes, it's nice if it's a good, close game, but, really, that's incidental. To use a word that's gone out of vogue, the Super Bowl succeeds because it's a *happening*, rather than a competition.

When the World Series ruled in the first half of the twentieth century, it was an altogether different attraction. Very few Americans had ever seen a big-league game, but there were only a few teams, and fans were familiar with their rosters. World Series games were inconveniently scheduled in the daytime—and most of them on workdays. It didn't come easy. You had to work to catch the Series.

Really, it was perverse. Americans knew the baseball players better, even if they had to imagine them. The World Series was mythic, whereas the Super Bowl is spectacle.

But then, that squares with the way the world has changed. We have grown more tangible and more literal. We're convinced the colors are more vivid on the screen than in our lives.

But however glitzy and surface, the Super Bowl squeezes us out of our niches and brings us together. At least for one afternoon it nurtures fellowship and instills a oneness in a people who are otherwise flying off in so many directions.

In that sense, Super Bowl Sunday is more genuinely a national holiday than some of those which are listed, officially, in the almanac.

For all the vulgarity and commercialism that goes with the Super Bowl, there is that coming together which is rare and sweet.

Play a Fore

1995

These are the differences between golfers and tennis players:

Golfers actually love to brag, masochistically, about how much time and effort they must commit merely to get to the course. "Me and Chuck got up at 3:30 just to be able to get to Pine Crest at 4:30 to sign up for a ten o'clock tee time. We didn't get home till four." Tennis players, in contrast, boast how easy it is to play quickly. "I skipped lunch yesterday so Howie and I could squeeze in two sets, but we were back at two for the budget session."

Professional golf is played by middle-aged men and old men. Professional tennis is played by young men and adolescent girls.

Golf fans are unbelievably positive. They cheer every shot. Even when they can't see where a drive is going, their instinct is to cheer. "Oooooh! Ahhhh. You da man." Tennis fans assume that every break of serve is a choke. Nobody ever wins. It's just: who chokes the most. Greg Norman couldn't have lasted five minutes in tennis.

Golfers are consumers. Tennis players are skinflints.

Golfers study golf magazines, which are the size of encyclopedias, and every month pick out new thousand-dollar kryptonite irons and helium balls. Tennis players skim over the rare advertisements in their slim tennis magazines and then go play with their trusty twenty-seven-year-old racket, which has (at least) five more good years in it.

Golfers remember—and discuss—every shot they ever made. "On sixteen, I took a seven when I shoulda used a six, so it found the trap and . . ." Tennis players think in the aggregate. "My backhand sucks . . ."

Golfers absolutely believe in golf balls. They talk as if these balls have independent control over them. If a golfer hits a bad shot, he always says that the ball—not his shot, but the ball—*found* the rough. Golf balls somehow always find bad places to go on their own. Tennis players say, "Hey, who brought the balls?"

Golf journalists want desperately to themselves play on the course where the pros are playing. Tennis journalists want to find out who the pros are sleeping with.

Golfers who hit long are exciting. Tennis players who hit hard are boring. Pete Sampras was born to be a golfer.

Golfers look good in golf clothes, so long as they carry a club. Tennis players manage to look bad in tennis clothes because they stick the extra balls in their pockets or underwear and look all lumpy.

Basically, people play golf so they can bet during a round and drink afterward, while . . . people play tennis so they can tell you they're in better shape than all the people who play golf.

Home Alone

2010

I have the odd sense that what was falsely feared more than half a century ago may be finally coming true now.

When television was new sports team owners were intuitively afraid that if you put games out there for people to see for free they wouldn't pay to come out to see the game in person. The NFL was praised to the heavens for having the wisest, restricted TV policy.

But as time went on, all that changed; the revised wisdom was that far from stunting the growth of live attendance, television whetted the appetite. You wanted to go out and be a part of what you'd gotten a taste of on TV. And cleaner stadiums, more comfortable seats, luxury suites, more convenient parking, and dedicated public transit made it even more attractive to *come on out!*

Not only did sports crowds increase tremendously, but owners also got paid more from the TV networks fighting over the chance to televise sports. By now whole generations have grown up expecting every game to be at the beck and call of our clicker. And games televise so clear and gorgeous. Living color? TV clarity today is better than mere life—it's heavenly.

Football, which televises best, has seen NFL ratings go higher than ever.

So I think we're seeing the beginning of a sea change in custom and habit. That's probably accelerated, too, because the owners—this will come as a shock, I know—have grown more greedy, and even rich fans are balking at buying seats that have Tiffany price tags. How often do you see games on TV where the best seats are the ones that are empty? That's something altogether new.

But even more important, younger fans have been raised on TV and other electronic entertainment. These are people who play video games by themselves for fun and who don't communicate so much face-to-face, but via text and Facebook. We thought that you had to be *at* the location to watch something "in person." To younger people today, what's "in person" is wherever *their* person is.

Besides, everybody has access to huge, brilliant high-definition TV. A Nielsen survey has shown, in fact, that sports events are watched by 21 percent more viewers if they have HD. I've talked to folks who've been on the sidelines at the huge, new Dallas Cowboys stadium, and, they say, people down there close to the field nevertheless choose to look away from the live-action game and watch on the monster video screens above.

Jerry Jones didn't build a stadium. He built the world's largest sports bar.

Then, too, especially with those games where bad weather is a factor, the urge to stay, as they say, in the comfort of your own home increases exponentially.

It's revealing that the movie studios now are anxious to get theatrical movies available at home sooner than ever before. Why go to the cinemaplex when you can go downstairs to your own entertainment center? That's the style people have grown up with. And hey, 3-D makes it ever better.

It seems obvious to me that the appeal of traveling to pay to be an eyewitness is being edged out by staying put and being comfortable. And when Internet betting is legalized, it'll be much more convenient to gamble at home. The roar of the crowd is so yesterday.

EIGHT

Match Play

2001

As we all know, the American male has survived wars, depression, fluoride in the water, and the emancipation of women—only to be brought down by golf. Hordes of our formerly finest now scatter across the landscape from dawn to dusk, leaving their wives and children behind, abandoning the vaunted American work ethic, going to hell—not in a handbasket, as we were always warned, but in a motorized cart.

One offshoot of this links mania has been the proliferation of golf magazines, and as I was staring at these myriad glossy publications the other day, I noticed how incredibly similar they were to women's magazines—which, of course, men have always made fun of. Look in the mirror, boys. Here are, alternating (and verbatim), titles from this month's women's and golf magazines:

CONFESSIONS OF A PRETTY WOMAN:
YOU CAN ONLY GET BY ON YOUR LOOKS

TIGER WOODS:
WE TELL HIM HOW TO GET EVEN BETTER

THE 25 SECRET SEX WISHES RACING
THROUGH HIS MIND

40 WAYS TO TAKE YOUR GAME TO NEW HEIGHTS

TOP 10 SWIMSUIT DON'TS

MAKE SURE YOUR SHORTS STILL FIT

THE NEW SEXUAL REVOLUTION—
LESS FREEDOM. MORE FUN

SINFULLY GOOD GOLF—IN UTAH

BURN FAT FASTER

RESTORE YOUR LOST POWER,
DISTANCE AND ACCURACY

HOW TO COPE WITH A KINKY BOYFRIEND

BE A BETTER PUTTER WHILE HAVING FUN

DESPERATE FOR A DIAMOND:
WOMEN WHO HAVE IT ALL EXCEPT THE PROPOSAL

LOUSY SWING SYNDROME:
IT COULD NEVER HAPPEN TO A PRO . . . COULD IT?

GET YOUR BEST HAIR EVER:
NEW TIPS AND TRICKS

CONSISTENT SPINE ANGLE IS YOUR SWING AXIS

A BIG "OHHH" EVERY TIME:
HOW TO FEEL FIREWORKS IN FIVE EASY STEPS

50 WAYS YOU CAN GET STRONGER AND LONGER

SEDUCE-ME MAKEOVERS

THE PRICE OF A PERFECT GREEN

PREP RALLY:
PULL OUT THE PINK, TURN UP YOUR COLLAR AND
CINCH YOUR WAIST WITH A RIBBON BELT

SHOW US YOUR WEDGE

A GOOD GIRL'S DARK SECRETS

CUT OUT SILLY THREE-PUTTS BEFORE YOU TEE OFF

GET BEAUTIFULLY BARE

THE ULTIMATE POWER MUSCLE

TEN MINUTES TO GORGEOUS

5 TOP PGA PROFESSIONALS SHOW YOU HOW TO MAKE
BIG IMPROVEMENTS IN JUST 10 MINUTES

REACH THE DEEPEST LEVEL OF LOVE

YOU WILL BREAK 90

Maybe there's not that much difference between us after all. Except women want to be better looking, better lovers, and better dressed—they want to be better women. Men just want to be better golfers.

Up to Speed

2005

I hold no particular brief for Fisher DeBerry, the football coach at the Air Force Academy who has tried in the past to make his young American cadets into a sort of gridiron version of Jesus's apostles. To be kind, Coach DeBerry is just not a real savvy guy, and last week after Air Force was whipped by Texas Christian, he allowed as how the winners, quote, "had a lot more African American players than we did, and they ran a lot faster than we did. It's obvious to me they run extremely well." For these remarks, DeBerry was taken to the woodshed by the head of the academy, and then, all but wearing sackcloth and ashes, he offered an abject apology for being "hurtful to many people."

Rather, what DeBerry should have apologized for was not being canny enough to speak in the euphemistic code that coaches and other members of the sporting brotherhood have come to guilelessly employ in talking about race. There is not a single person who has even a nodding acquaintance with sports who does not know that in DeBerry's game of football, at the most accomplished levels, virtually all the speed positions, defensive backs, running backs, and wide receivers, are filled with African American players. Likewise in basketball, in the backcourt, or more simply, virtually all

Olympic-level sprints have for decades been won by black runners.

I myself do not pretend to know why this is so. I am not a physiologist, an anthropologist, or a sociologist. Authorities in genetics, culture, and history have all presented various explanations. I don't know. But I am not blind, and I simply see what everybody does, that when it comes to speed in the top echelons, these positions are filled almost entirely by black athletes. Within sport, everybody casually acknowledges this. When coaches pragmatically observe that they need more speed or "better athletes," everybody understands that this means recruiting African Americans. Players themselves, white or black, have joked for years about "white man's disease." The movie *White Men Can't Jump* could hardly have been more transparent. Comedians of all races tell jokes on the subject. So we can laugh about the situation. We all talk about it in private, but the instant somebody like the artless DeBerry says out loud what everybody blithely accepts, even jokes about, the sports community turns on him and castigates him. It's bad enough that there is so much hypocrisy surrounding the subject. When it is embroidered with sanctimony, it becomes sickening.

You know, in matters of race, we have a hard enough time dealing with the subject without pretending. If we can't be honest with ourselves about issues that are obvious and really inconsequential in the full scheme of things, then how in the world are we ever going to confront what is complex and important about race?

Did He Say That?

2005

I suppose folks would say Muhammad Ali is the most famous athlete living in this country; well, possibly Michael Jordan. But then when I saw a certain someone the other day, it occurred to me, you know, there may be another American sportsman who keeps coming back into our consciousness more than any other. Think about it when I say the name, Yogi Berra. Right?

"Listen up. I've got nothing to say, so I'm only going to say it once." Yogi just recently had his eightieth birthday. "I want to thank you for making this day necessary." But he's part of our culture, isn't he, in ways that other great athletes never manage. Yogi remains the ultimate in athletic Americana.

It isn't just that he succeeded Gracie Allen for being the best at saying perfect things so imperfectly. "Nobody goes there anymore. It's too crowded." Neither is it said that he's that rarest human being to have had a cartoon character named after him, the irrepressible Yogi Bear.

No, Yogi was so endearing from the first, even before we heard him mangle the language, because we could identify with him. He was the Yankee you rooted for even if you hated the Yankees. So many athletes are tall and handsome, buffed. Berra was no more than five eight, a blocky 195 pounds with a countenance that, well, left even the most generous beholders hard-pressed to find beauty. "So what? I never saw anyone hit with his face."

He was just as fabulous behind the plate, catching, as he was beside it, swinging. He knew the game intuitively, smart enough as a manager to win pennants in both the American and the National Leagues. So what if he said goofy things? "It gets late early out here."

Probably, too, he didn't utter quite all that's been attributed to him or, as Yogi himself explained it, "I didn't really say everything I said." But, hey, it took Sheridan to make up Mrs. Malaprop and give us malapropism. Lawrence Peter Berra gave us Yogiism all by himself. But you knew that already, didn't you? So, of course, excuse me, "It's déjà vu all over again."

Yogi was back at Cooperstown last week, one of the oldest living Hall of Famers. "It ain't over till it's over." As he enters his eighties, nature's nobleman, he's trimmer than when he played, balding, bespectacled, wizened. Who would believe that this little old man schmoozing with all the sturdy big guys came out of World War II, bobbing in the waves, dodging the artillery, in a little thirty-six-foot boat off of Normandy, to become one of the finest athletes of his era—not to mention then going on to become something of a national treasure?

Good to see you again, Yogi, still being Yogi. Or if you do say so yourself, "If you can't imitate him, don't copy him."

Da Boys Will Be Boys

2006

By now, all our schoolboys and schoolgirls are back in the little red schoolhouses, studying diligently. Well, the schoolgirls are.

Books have been written, like *The War Against Boys*, to suggest that American schools are set up to favor girls. And there's even talk that we need affirmative action to help these intellectually handicapped boys. Or if not, we're going to end up with an American society of eggheaded executive woman and ham-headed worker men, where the gals do all the heavy thinking while the guys come home from their jobs flipping burgers and spend their downtime playing video games and watching poker and arena football on TV.

This fall, 58 percent of the U.S. college population will be female, and more women stay in college and more apply all the time. When this freshman class graduates in 2010, the Department of Education estimates that as many as three out of every five diplomas may very well go to women.

Now there are a lot of reasons which may account for this, including the dread possibility that the weaker sex, so-called, may be, well, simply smarter than we dim brutes. But I certainly think that at least some of this scholastic imbalance may be accounted for by the fact that, from an early age, boys are directed toward sports and rewarded more for their athletic prowess than for their classroom work.

It isn't either just that classic inner-city delusion where little boys bet their futures on becoming great multimillionaire sports superstars. No, in our middle classes all too many parents push children to excel in sport so that their child might win a college athletic scholarship.

This is the cockeyed system we've developed in the United States wherein the free road to a college education is through a tennis court or a soccer field, while someone more accomplished in the school classroom has a harder time getting into the college classroom.

How else do colleges desperately try to attract more males? Well, even for those geeks who can't play a sport, more and more colleges offer sports management courses. Yes sirree, Bob! We're going to have the best-run sports franchises in the world. Of course they'll all be owned by people from India and China. And women.

Another desperate admissions ploy is for small colleges to field football teams. It's much the costliest sport around, but football is a game played virtually only by men, so that helps to artificially inflate that shrinking male college ratio.

Well, there is one hope for us guys. Because of Title IX, more and more girls are being introduced to sports. And studies show that female athletes eventually start to act like their male colleagues. That is, their grades go down, and they lose interest in other campus activity.

Here's our chance, men. Don't protest Title IX; support it! Get those little girls away from their homework and out on the playground with us! It may be our only hope to keep running America in the style to which we fellows are accustomed.

Time to Go

2011

Every star in every sport who is getting a little long in the tooth ought to be told what happened exactly seventy-six years ago today. Babe Ruth hit three home runs, the last a monstrous blast that soared out of the stadium itself.

Wow—what a performance for a guy who was forty years old.

But here's the more important truth: five days later, Ruth played his last game. He was finished.

Athletes, you see, do not decline on a gentle, sloping curve. Rather, their skills wither jaggedly, so it's not uncommon for a fading hero to suddenly have one day when he plays as if he were back in the prime of his youth, a marvel once again. I've seen it so often.

But alas, it's only an accident of odds, an evening's triumph of muscle memory over athletic actuarial. The next day, the next game, age wins again. Only of course, the athlete has been seduced by the aberration: "See, I've still got it."

It's so hard for anybody who's been extraordinary at something glamorous, as thousands cheer, to admit, as a relatively young person, "Now I'm passing on, too, just as even Babe Ruth did once."

It's an even more difficult concession to make now in base-ball, because, with performance-enhancing drugs, so many baseball players recently seemed to have Ponce de León as an agent.

Now, as always, we can see through the glass, darkly, that some of the best are in various stages of decline.

Kobe Bryant was clearly a diminished presence for the Lakers in the playoffs, as Roger Federer has dropped down a step from the top of tennis. Could he win another major? Sure, if Federer got a good draw and got that one old-fashioned great performance in the finals. Maybe Tiger Woods can, too—if his lower body isn't as battered as are his emotions.

The most attention has been paid to Derek Jeter, whose celebrated slump actually made a front-page story in the *New York Times*. He then hit two homers in one game, though, and that seemed to convince Jeter and a lot of other folks that he had miraculously shucked off his baseball dotage.

But no: in all sports, the irrefutable models show again and again that once age begins to affect a player, the die is cast.

It takes a rare beast to accept that, though. Maybe the best example took place twenty-two years ago this week. Mike Schmidt of the Phillies, age thirty-nine, the greatest third base-man ever to play the game, had, for that time, a huge con-tract. But after just forty-two games that season, he simply quit. Schmidt said bluntly, "I no longer have the skills."

But how rare it is for great players to admit that they've lost the talent they've had all their wondrous lives.

So just that one good day—every now and then—is a pow-erful cocktail to sustain the illusion: "See, I've still got it."

But he doesn't.

A Good Aim

2012

I've never had any interest in hunting. Among other things, I'm a terrible shot, but I have friends who hunt, and it appears to me to be a perfectly reasonable hobby—certainly every bit as honorable as fantasy football. Moreover, shooting a deer or a duck with a bullet seems to me no more inhumane than catching a trout or a marlin with a hook.

Oh, sometimes I get a little piqued that those who hunt and fish are ennobled as "sportsmen," while people who play golf are just golfers and people who bowl are just bowlers. But then, that's just me being picayune.

As the nation becomes less rural, there are, predictably, fewer sportsmen; but still, today, there are at least thirteen million hunters in the United States. This is almost three times the number of Americans who are members of the National Rifle Association, and, of course, many members of the NRA are sportsmen.

So now, we contemplate yet another mass gun murder—at a school where someone I know sometimes works. These massacres are so commonplace by now that it's only a lucky degree of separation for us all, isn't it?

But notwithstanding President Obama's impassioned promise to reform our gun laws, we know how our craven politicians invariably proceed: they dramatically decry the violence, conspicuously pray for the victims, and then do absolutely nothing because they are lobotomized by the fear that the NRA will wail that our Second Amendment rights are being abrogated, so that then these one-issue voters will throw them out of office.

All this is old hat, so there is no sense struggling with what exactly James Madison had in mind about the militia when he and his otherwise succinct brethren were marking up the Bill of Rights. Nor do we need to hear how no laws can stop crazy people from getting guns, so what's the point of gun laws in our nation or laws for everything else? And how guns don't kill people, and so on and so forth.

Rather, it's just obvious that we Americans possess too many firearms—almost ninety per one hundred people, far more than anybody else in the whole world. And obviously it's too easy for us to obtain these automatic weapons of human destruction—*this* should also be obvious by now—and that nothing will change unless the very people who *are* gun owners themselves support the changes the president swears to promote. Hunters are good citizens who want guns to shoot game. Nobody can accuse *them* of supporting the confiscation of guns.

If the sportsmen would let their voices of conscience be heard above the homicidal fusillade, then some sensible prohibitions could be enacted, for those who have the potential to reduce the gun carnage in the United States of America are precisely the people who own guns and who are good sports.

Deliverance

2013

As a child, your heart is broken when you learn that there's no tooth fairy. If you're a baseball fan, that disillusionment happens once more to you in life when you first hear the numbers mavens tell you that there is no such thing as a clutch hitter. None. No such thing.

Oh my, but if you have any romance in your soul, you do so want to believe that there are people in all walks of life whom we can count on to rise to the occasion. Don't you want that?

But at least since 1977, when a statistics scholar named Dick Cramer came up with figures that showed that no batter in baseball did consistently better in a pressure situation than he did in his everyday at bats, no other study has disputed that conclusion. So, if you don't go along with the raw figures you're left with: faith, Benjamin Disraeli, and Derek Jeter.

Faith says: I still believe that some of us are more valiant than the rest.

Benjamin Disraeli once said: "There are three kinds of lies: lies, damned lies, and statistics."

Derek Jeter said: "You can take those stats guys and throw them out the window."

But stats guys are hard-hearted brutes, they are. And especially now at World Series time, far from going out the window, they come out of the woodwork to make sure that we silly dreamers understand that numbers don't lie, that the clutch is all a random crapshoot. You can't count on nobody nohow.

Okay, I'm a wide-eyed sucker. The trouble with the numbers is that they tell us that all baseball players and—therefore, by extension—all human beings respond exactly the same to pressure. And we know that's not true. There was never a basketball team I was close to that the coach or players didn't tell me that certain teammates didn't want the ball at the end of a close game and others craved it. Numbers? These were guys who knew the heart and soul of their fellows. They knew there was a difference in the desire that nurtured success.

Are we to believe that baseball players are any different? Granted, wanting to get up to the plate in the clutch and succeeding thereupon are two different things. But do we really believe that everybody will respond the same in the crucible? Does everybody also try the same? Care the same? Love the same?

It's always hard to refute the numbers, especially when those zealots who swear by them are so dismissive of the old stick-in-the-muds who can't see that numerical equations are sacraments. But I'm sorry. I want to believe in old-fashioned human nature, too.

It's revealing that when somebody gets a big hit, we invariably say: he delivered. Fool that I am, I still think some of us can deliver better than ever when the chips are down, the count is full, and the game is on the line.

NINE

Who Needs War?

2011

It's the start of the football season again, just as the war in Iraq officially ends and the one in Afghanistan proceeds. And, as always, there's the old cliché that football is a benign substitute for war: ground attacks, flanks, bombs, blitzes, and so forth.

But it *is* a truth, not a cliché, that our football has gained in popularity in the United States as we have had less success with our wars. It makes me wonder if, ironically, football doesn't provide us more with *nostalgia* for the way war used to be—with clear battle maps, focused campaigns, and simple battle lines.

And, of course, football games have neat conclusions—they're simply won or lost. But our wars are precisely *not* settled that way anymore; their goals are vague and imprecise and they just drag on and on, without resolution.

So, ultimately, given our shallow attention span, war bores us, and since so few of us citizens are asked to actively be engaged in our war, most of us are merely citizen-spectators to it, rather than compatriots, and, in this television world today, we lose interest in war. Football is better to watch.

Of course, all that aside, the increased popularity of football may be explained by the fact that it has become so much more violent than our other team sports . . . as indeed we prefer more violence in most all phases of our entertainment today. Mixed martial arts is more violent than traditional boxing, auto racing is more violent than horse racing, and professional wrestling makes comedy out of brutality. Our movies and television shows, too, are more violent, and our children grow up devoted to incredibly bloodthirsty video games. Even our music, that which soothes a savage breast, is more savage today.

It's been glib to say that violence in America is as traditional as apple pie. I don't think so. The new violence is showbiz. Rather than traditional, it's trendy—a fashionably entertaining part of everyday life, not any by-product of our aggressive heritage. And for all the beautiful excitement in football—the spectacular kickoff returns, the long touchdown passes—the one constant is the hitting. We very much enjoy watching football players hit one another. That makes the highlight reel.

The NFL has belatedly begun to acknowledge that the potential for damage to athletes' minds and bodies is probably much more the case than we have been prepared to admit. It is almost as if we didn't want to recognize that in a sport where hits to the head are so common, concussions are bound to happen. But then, since we no longer pay that much attention to our wars, it's easy to overlook casualties there, as well. Football and war today seem to have that in common, too.

Headmaster

2005

An ode to baseball caps. Oh, baseball cap—I know. I know. Why in the world are you talking about baseball caps at all, let alone in December, when it isn't baseball season? But, you see, that's exactly the point. Baseball caps are now bigger than baseball. Around the world, they now may well even be the most familiar American artifact—passing Coca-Cola and blue jeans and bad movies.

Think about it. How many baseball caps actually end up on the heads of baseball players? Well, I'd wager that fewer people with baseball caps play baseball than do people in tennis shoes play tennis or people in Polo shirts play polo. Not only that, but baseball caps have risen to preeminence at a time when headgear in general has been in decline. The fedora has gone the way of spats. The beret remains the favorite choice of a few noggins, but as sure as English has replaced French as the language of diplomacy, so has the baseball cap swamped the beret sur la tête, the final indignity to Gallic pride.

Baseball caps have become ubiquitous, largely because women have taken to them, too. Name another hat that is so unisexual. This is largely because of the most brilliant clothing invention since the zipper, namely the hole in the rear of the baseball cap so that ladies might let their glorious long locks stream through the gap in the cap, absolutely Dr. Seussian.

Actually, I'll bet you never thought of this. We shouldn't be surprised that women now wear baseball caps because as millinery experts have divined, the baseball cap in shape and utility is closest to the old-fashioned Victorian sunbonnet. Visualize that now, right? And it also helps the hegemony of baseball caps that they have the adjuster with the little holes in the back. This way, one size fits all. I have a pinhead. I had an old friend with a noggin the size of a watermelon. We called him the head of the school, but the two of us can buy the exact same baseball cap, for men's heads, women's heads, big heads, little heads. The baseball cap may be the most universal article of clothing ever designed.

One of the ironic things about baseball caps is that so many people in other sports wear them. Tennis players and golfers wear baseball caps when they're playing tennis and golf. Football quarterbacks put them on as soon as they take off their helmets, so, too, automobile racers. I don't understand, though, why so many people wear baseball caps backward. This doesn't keep the sun out of your eyes and the gap in the cap looks foolish on your forehead. Of course, a few young knuckleheads even wear baseball caps sort of sideways. Whatever. What you don't see much of anymore is folks who wear their baseball caps way back up on the head. These are the types who tend to scratch their heads. That seems to have mostly gone out. Oh, it'll probably come back in style, though.

Baseball caps have clearly become the prime fashion of the twenty-first-century world.

Girl Watching

2009

The Ladies Professional Golf Association is like the NAACP: both are a bit retro in their language.

Nobody says "colored people" anymore, and, at least in sports, "ladies" is passé. Apart from golf, the females playing professionally today are not L's, but W's—women: the WTA, the WNBA, and so forth. After the old joke: that is no lady, that's my athlete.

Unfortunately, across the board, in sports, these raw economic times have hit women harder. We must remember that women's sports, like women's colleges, operate at a disadvantage when it comes to attracting the big money that is so often controlled by men.

But also this: whether it's cultural or genetic or both, women do not seem as inclined as men to pay to watch their own gender play games.

Nothing illustrated this better than the Women's United Soccer Association, which opened in 2001 in the afterglow of the U.S. team's World Cup victory, but folded ingloriously only two years later after a loss of $100 million.

Meanwhile, the WNBA limps along, forced to play as something of a basketball afterthought in the summer. The

WNBA's Houston franchise is so far the only to fold in any major sport since the great recession began. Then, earlier this month, as ladies' golf kept bleeding sponsors, the LPGA forced out its commissioner.

And, of course, sexism still raises its ugly head—or, some would say, its pretty head. There was the recent brouhaha when a Wimbledon official admitted, rather blithely, that often the choice of which female players were scheduled on the show courts had more to do with looks than talent.

Everybody was aghast at such overt chauvinism, only the harsh reality is that until women start stepping up and buying tickets for women's games, then—like it or not—sex may simply be good at the box office.

Ten years later, what do most people remember about the 1999 World Cup—that Brandi Chastain scored the winning goal? No, that Brandi Chastain took her shirt off.

American school sports also have had to cut back, although the men in charge invariably make efforts to preserve football at all costs. Aha, but Title IX requires proportionate athletic representation, and football is so manpower intensive that this, ipso facto, threatens the existence of other boys' sports.

And here's the greater irony: as American girls outdo boys in the classroom, more girls go to college. If boys like watching sports that much more than studying, fine. That's all they'll be doing—watching—because college teams will, increasingly, by law, be women's teams. I'm not being facetious when I say that college athletic programs are heading toward a time when the men's side may be football and basketball alone, while women will have a wide array of sports to choose from.

Someday, too, women may even go watch some of the games that other women play.

Too Much to Care

1996

Ironically, even as Michael Jordan's agent asks for the kind of money that *Twister* has been taking in at the box office, salaries really don't matter that much anymore. Oh sure, to the players and their agents and the owners, it's still a way of doing business. But while the fans may still think that professional athletes are unworthy lucky devils, the money that players are paid now is so incredible that, for fans, it's become meaningless.

On the other hand, when players were making salaries that could be related to what the average working stiff made, fans had very strong opinions on salaries, and could, often as not, be unforgiving, even of their own team's players' salaries.

Some player would ask for a $5,000 raise to $35,000 a year and fans would say: "Whoa, he only hit .293, and he only drove in eighty-three runs and look at what other third basemen did—so where does he come off thinking he's due thirty-five? Thirty-two-five should be just fine, thank you."

When Sandy Koufax and Don Drysdale banded together thirty years ago to try to break through the $100,000 glass ceiling, fans everywhere—prominently including Dodger fans—were . . . well, they were offended. There prevailed the view then that we were all sort of in this together—player, team, league, fan—and that if somebody made too much it'd somehow throw this whole delicate mechanism off balance.

You see, in the matter of players' salaries, we average Joes could relate to them. If you were making $18,200 yourself, then you had a sense of what $35,000 meant to a player. At a time when I was earning about $10,000, I can vividly recall going into the Yankees' clubhouse after the 1963 World Series and passing on the news to a couple of friends of mine on the team that their losing share might very well come to as much as $8,500 a man. I was as thrilled for them as I was envious. We all understood what $8,500 meant.

But now, today, when somebody asks me if I think Alonzo Mourning is worth $17 million a year, I have no more response than if somebody requested my views on whether or not they should raise import taxes in Luxembourg by a quarter of a percent.

What is Michael Jordan worth? What is a breeze worth on a summer's day? What is a smile worth? Who knows? Jordan is worth a certain amount to the Bulls as a player at their box office. He is worth a certain amount to other teams when he comes to their towns. He is worth a certain amount to the NBA's television contract to the Philippines. How much? Who knows?

Never mind Jordan. For any player, with salary caps, balloon payments, deferred payments, bonuses—who knows? At a certain point, fans simply stopped being involved emotionally in how much any player made, and as the numbers grew it became even more difficult to even understand the figures, academically. In an odd way, some kind of visceral connection was lost between the fan and the player when money no longer became a personal issue.

Rather today, basically, the fans just want their owner to pay whatever it takes to get a player or to keep him—while they will rail on about how everybody else's players are overpaid. But it is a hollow harping. Our hearts aren't in it anymore. Neither, even, is our bile. We don't know if Alonzo Mourning is worth $17 million, and frankly, my dear, we don't give a damn.

Namesake

2003

I don't know why, but I'm always intrigued by sports nicknames. Why, for example, aren't there ever any major-league
teams named after dogs? Meanwhile, there are lots of bird
teams. Maybe it's because if you name your team, say, the Ter-
riers or the Hounds, then when they play poorly, you know all
the headlines will say "Going to the Dogs" or "Dogging It"
and stuff like that. Or explain this to me: virtually all the teams
that have two words in their nicknames or two distinct names
in one word, like Redskins, are always known by the last name;
that is, the Red Wings are always the Wings, the Supersonics
the Sonics, the 49ers the Niners, and so forth.

Why is this always so? For example, why aren't the Cowboys called the Cows instead of the Boys and why aren't the
Mighty Ducks called the Mightys instead of the Ducks? However, when teams have only a one-word nickname and it is
shortened, it's invariably called by the first syllable: the Pats, the
Avs, the Cavs. The Astros are the one major exception to this
rule. The Astros are called the Stros. I'll let you figure out why.

The best contracted nicknames are the ChiSox and the
BoSox. They're my favorites. D-Backs is a late entry, and I think
I like D-Backs, but why not the Diamonds? Well, Diamonds,

you see, is a first name. A few nicknames produce their own group nicknames. I like these. Flock for the various birds, Tribe for the Indians, Fish for the Dolphins and Marlins. Do they ever say Pack for the Timberwolves or Herd for the Rams? Rams do come in herds, don't they? How about Nobility for the Royals? Nobility top Flock. Or Clergy for the Padres. Clergy edge Tribe. I like that.

A few teams have nicknames for the nicknames. The Canadians are the Habs, the Angels the Halos, the hockey Rangers the Blues, the Yankees the Bronx Bombers. I think the Cubs have the only real diminutive, the Cubbies. That's what happens when you lose all the time. The Ottawa Senators are called the Sens, but when Washington had the Senators, they were never the Sens. Sometimes, though, the Washington Senators were called the Nationals, because it could be shortened more affectionately to Nats, even if that reminds you of bugs. Anyway, one year, they had a slogan in Washington, "I'm crazy about the Senators, but I'm nuts about the Nats." Unfortunately, the Nats lost just as often as the Senators.

No team should be allowed to take its nickname when it leaves town. I was so glad that Cleveland kept the Browns, but then: the Utah Jazz, the Los Angeles Lakers, the Memphis Grizzlies? Nonsense. A new town, a new nickname—that should be a constitutional amendment. For perversity, though, my favorite nickname is the Atlanta Falcons. In the Middle Ages, when falconry was popular with the royals—no, not the Kansas City Royals—the falcons used for hunting were females. Male falcons were smaller, weaker, and not as pretty as the females. They were called tiercels. Each Sunday when the Falcons of Atlanta lose another football game, I always wonder, do the players know they're named after girls?

The Patriots Act

2004

Certain sports possess major cultural qualities—even if they're contradictory. Football, for example, is both militaristic and social, a brutal game of field generals and platoons and bombs, surrounded by weekend party conviviality—dates and drinks, tailgating and bared-midriff sexy cheerleaders.

That martial side of football also increasingly highlights the technological. Coaches are all attached by telephones; assistants use camera surveillance; computers are as much a part of the game now as are shoulder pads and painkillers. No team is more advanced than the New England Patriots.

More important, it is as much the methods that the Patriots use off the field to build their team as it is their style on the field that make them the juggernaut they have improbably become in a league that is supposed to be all about parity.

The four-star general who commands the Patriots is their head coach, Bill Belichick, a man with a background that might seem at odds with coaching. As a player, Belichick was better at lacrosse than football. He attended an elite prep school, Andover; and then Wesleyan College, with its Division-III football program. But Belichick was also the son of a football coach at the Naval Academy, so he grew up in both a football and a military environment.

Presumably Belichick is a fine coach on the field, but in a way, we don't really know. Or even: maybe it doesn't matter. We do know that he has superb assistants. Football, like the army, is a hierarchical enterprise.

Staff officers are crucial. And just as crucially, Belichick has developed a system to deal with the bureaucratic intricacies of the business of football today, where the salary cap and free agency force complicated commercial decisions on all franchises.

It is Belichick's ability to manipulate personnel and finances that has primarily made the Patriots the winner of a record twenty straight games. Management executives and academics see Belichick more as a CEO than a coach.

This developed sophistication in football is something that seems to leap ahead once a generation. There have been lots of outstanding teams through the years, but Belichick's Patriots are specifically the heirs of the postwar Cleveland Browns and the 1970s Dallas Cowboys.

The Browns were actually named for their domineering coach, Paul Brown. He made football coaching more organized and modern, showing how valuable game films could be. He infuriated traditionalists by using what were called "messenger guards," to send in all plays from the bench. Two decades later, the Cowboys organization, under a general manager named Tex Schramm, took scouting to new heights of engagement— while, in tandem, introducing glamorous cheerleaders and other up-to-date marketing advances.

Like Belichick, both Paul Brown and Tom Landry, the Cowboys' coach, were dry and colorless characters—the antithesis of the classic emotional model of the American football coach—the Knute Rockne, Vince Lombardi, Bear Bryant type.

But as Brown's and Landry's franchises eventually influenced all their rivals, so have Belichick's Patriots begun to change the way other NFL teams operate.

The Patriots are bound to lose sometime this season. They may very well not even win the Super Bowl again. But whatever happens, the twenty-first-century organization man, Belichick, has made the Patriots the bellwether franchise of this NFL generation, just as the Browns and Cowboys were in their time.

The Forgotten
(Well, Briefly)

1997

We are now about to enter that strange quadrennial phase, when, all of a sudden, the United States of America, the world's only superpower, finds itself on the dark side of the moon . . . while the rest of the world goes bonkers over the World Cup.

That's soccer, the bizarre sport you purposely play without the use of your hands—the very things that raised humankind above the beasts of the field.

And you wonder why we're the world's only superpower.

Already the mad disease is sweeping the globe. The usual riots in South America. In England, a poll of young men found that 95 percent of them would rather watch a World Cup game—even if just on television—than make love to "the woman of their dreams." And you thought they were nutty in Green Bay, Wisconsin.

And, as much as all the world points its toes for the Germans and the Brazilians, the perennial powers on the soccer pitch, for now the antipathy has been pointed at the French, who are hosting the cup this time around. Four years ago, in an unsuccessful effort to stir up interest in heathen America, the

World Cup was played in our huge stadiums here, with mini-
mum domestic interest. But now, in France, the stadiums are
petite and the European ticket demands are sky-high. When
the French finally put some ducats on sale for the rest of the
world, it quickly became impossible even to get through to the
box office on the telephone.

In fact, it is approximately as difficult to buy a World Cup
seat as it is to score a goal in a World Cup game—which, invariably, ends one-nil. The rest of Europe went apoplectic at
the French. In typical British tabloid understatement, the *Daily
Star* declared: "A good kicking on their Gallic derriere is the
only language the greedy frogs understand."

But isn't it wonderful? When the World Cup is on, nobody
even thinks to complain about Americans.

For once, you see, we in the United States are basically out of
it. In everything else, we are out front, up to our ears—keeping
the peace, threatening war, enforcing agreements, stuffing the
UN, financing, pontificating, making movies, winning gold
medals.

But now, for once, we can be just like Sweden or Switzerland.
Oh, sure, we do have a team in the World Cup, but the only
people in the U.S. who care about soccer are those odd disparate extremes of rich suburbanites and newly arrived immigrants.
What a wonderful sitcom it would make—maybe it would even
replace *Seinfeld*—as the Junior League blonde just out of Welles-
ley falls for the uneducated, young Caribbean immigrant . . . at a
soccer game. It would be the nineties version of *Abie's Irish Rose*.

In the meantime, though, soccer belongs to the rest of the
world, and we are the only sane people around, using our hands
and our minds together, as God intended, so that we might
regain the world again as soon as the madness finally ends in
France in July.

TEN

All Guys All the Time

2011

As best I know, I own the distinction of being the first human being to call our national attention to a linguistic phenomenon.

This was back in 1972, in an article in *Sports Illustrated* about Robyn Smith, who was then the best female jockey in the land. Smith referred to married couples as "you guys." I was so bemused that someone might actually refer to a woman as a guy that I felt obliged to mention it in the piece.

So, that was thirty-nine years ago. But now, my friends, guy has just taken over. There are no men and women left, no males or females, let alone ladies and gentlemen or boys and girls. It's just guys. Even down South, "y'all" is being replaced by "you guys." Recently, even the president ended his press conference saying, "Thank you, guys."

How did females become guys? How did everyone become guys? Remember, too, that a male guy was something of a scoundrel. And a wise guy was a fresh kid, a whippersnapper. In its most famous other evocation, men in Brooklyn said "youse guys." Damon Runyon referred to hustlers, gamblers, and other nefarious types as guys.

Now every mother's son is a guy and every mother's daughter, too. If they wrote the musical now, it wouldn't be called *Guys and Dolls*—just *Guys and Guys*.

What accounts for the guy-ification of America? Maybe it has to do with the fact that men had to stop calling grown women "girls." Gals kind of went out, too, so there wasn't anything else available. In sports, for a long time, even after it was gauche for anyone else to call adult females "girls," female athletes still referred to each other as "girls," but that just won't do anymore.

Now, the only place where we allow females to remain forever young is where love is involved: girlfriends and (with males, too), boyfriends. We'll have reached the nadir when it's just guyfriends and guyfriends.

Now that guy has been appropriated by women, men have started to use "dude" a lot more, but that remains mostly in the singular, as a form of address, as "sir" used to be. For example, someone will say: "Yo, dude, who are the guys on your team?" Still, nobody addresses anybody as guy. We'll say: "Dude, you're a good guy," but nobody says: "Guy, you're a good dude."

Understand, I have nothing against women becoming guys, too. I'm just tired of everything being guy-ish. Now we're all just . . . guys. All guys are created equal. God is a guy now. Your father is just another guy. So is your mother. Guys, start your engines. Happy Valentine's, my guy. A pretty guy is like a melody. We're all the same guys under the skin.

Yo, dude, let's stop guying.

Loyal (Sports) Alumni

2002

Inasumuch as I'm not a drug dealer, gunrunner, white slaver, or Olympics figure skating judge, I've had little contact with the Russian Mafia, except for one evening a few years ago at a fine restaurant in St. Petersburg. My wife and I and another couple were ushered to a table and had just had our cocktails put before us when suddenly, the maître d', previously the most obsequious of men, scurried back over to us and desperately pleaded with us to move: Now, pronto, immediately! I could see that the poor man was nearly hysterical with fear, and since all he wanted was for us to go to the very next almost identical table, we were happy to comply.

The panic subsided from the maître d's face, but moments later, we saw the reason for his terror when who should show up but two big-time Russian hoods and their brassy molls. The table we four had been seated at was *their* table and, by God, they expected it. They plunked down, lit up big cigars, ordered the most expensive champagne, and reveled in their own glory. They had the best table in the house, and it mattered plenty. You bet it did.

I remembered this the other day when the international gendarmes figured a Russian crook for trying to fix the pairs

skating and ice dancing in Salt Lake City. Everybody chuck-
led at the patent nonsense of some thug fixing a figure skating
competition when there was no payoff, nothing in it for him.
What a bunch of Bolshevik hayseeds. But no, just as there are
people the world over who believe it is very important for them
to have the right table, so are there sports fans who care about
their team winning all that much. Often, as a matter of fact,
these are the same people. It meant so very much to that Russian hood for his country to win a gold medal.

You see, before we snicker at the Russians, we ought to think
about how many of our own sophisticated country-club Americans do exactly the same thing. These are men who often have
almost everything in life, including the best tables at restaurants,
but in order to help their college win football or basketball
games, they willingly lie, break rules. They pay players under
the table, contribute to slush funds, all for no gain for themselves,
just for the joy of seeing old State U win.

Our American booster Mafia is larger and every bit as egre-
giously dishonorable as the Russian Mafia. An Olympic gold or
a bowl game, it's all very much the same. It's not just the alumni
boosters either. There are college presidents who hire tainted
coaches, knowing these coaches will recruit bums. There are
admissions officers who let athletes in who don't quality. Then
there are professors who give passing grades to these athletes
just to keep them eligible. And nobody does this for any real
personal gain. It's just to share in the joy of our side winning.
But make no mistake, it's all a fix. It's breaking the rules to win.
Human nature is really very much the same when it comes to
athletics in this world. Don't put down the Russian gangster
just because he wants to win so much that he'll cheat and fina-
gle to do it. Look who's sitting at the same good table with him.
Often as not, it's our own American guys from your alma mater.

The Old Butterfly

2009

Muhammad Ali flew to England last week, there to make appearances in soccer stadiums. He said it would probably be his "last time" in the U.K. He can barely move on his own now. One London newspaper called Ali, who was once "a butterfly," "little more than a zombie." And a great many people find it as upsetting as it is sad that the old champ continues to make personal appearances.

Maybe it would've been best if our last image of him had been in '96, when he suddenly appeared out of nowhere and—already shaking terribly from Parkinson's—still managed to light the Olympic flame. There was a nobility to that scene, as if once more he'd gotten off the canvas, managed somehow to win another fight.

But Ali wouldn't retire from the ring when he should have, and now he refuses to comfort us and slip away from public view.

Perhaps there's a bolder statement in that, that the man who once so immodestly enjoyed standing before us—the laird of his realm, proclaiming his beauty to the heavens—is now unafraid to let us see him when his great body is slumped and shambling.

But might we be too tender with our memories? The athlete dying young has always seemed so shocking, so unfair—but I suspect that it upsets us even more to actually see our heroes, those physical marvels, grown old and infirm, as vulnerable to age and disease as we ordinary folk are. We want to remember the paragon, not the mere human.

Ah, but in contradiction, Ali's wife, Lonnie, speaks for her husband, saying that for as long as he can manage to travel and make silent appearances, it "is not just his living; it is his life." There must, for him, be as much in satisfaction as in remuneration that he can still command up to $100,000 just for showing up.

The busted old pug was long a stereotype in our athletic cavalcade. That Ali is broken—but not broke—is a certain ironic revenge. And he, who was once so reviled by so many Americans, has become quite a beloved figure in his dotage. Complicated as he has been, he won the fight for our affection, too.

I can so vividly remember, a few years ago, when a photographer I was with posed him before the Vietnam Veterans Memorial in Washington, D.C. I thought that was insane. Who, after all, was more identified with opposition to that war?

But when the people there—searching for the names of their loved ones who had died for what Ali opposed—when they spotted him, they rushed to him, even handed me their little cameras to take snapshots with him, embraced him. It was dear.

Even as boxing, as a sport, fades to the fringes, Muhammad Ali still retains some kind of hold on us. If he yet wants to present his present, lesser self to us, it is not for us to feel pity for him.

Sound Off

2004

Often, as I travel, I try to remember exactly why it was that people used to be so upset by Muzak, by elevator music. We didn't know how good we had it. Oh, as I move about now, what I would give just to be able to hear Mantovani playing "Moon River" again and again. Instead, our unwilling ears are now bombarded by all manner of speech, of announcements, of advisories and proscriptions, of radio and television programs.

When did it become official national policy that no public place could be allowed to exist without constant programmed noise?

And that, of course, doesn't even take into account the volunteer noisemakers who feel inclined to conduct their personal conversations, loudly, on cell phones. Excuse me: yell phones.

Alas, as an institution, sport is a prime accomplice in the modern crime of unmitigated noise. The worse thing about Janet Jackson baring her breast during the Super Bowl halftime show was that it diverted criticism away from the unrestrained cacophony that had preceded her unveiling. Surely, our ears were offended far worse than our eyes, but the NFL has escaped that censure.

But, of course, it is attending games where we are at greatest risk. Each year stadiums and arenas become artificially noisier, as the public-address system blares out trumpet calls and canned music and just plain loud racket. There used to be something so wonderfully pure about a crowd letting out a spontaneous roar. Now, unfortunately, fans are just as liable to, in unison, scream vulgarities. It is called free speech, although you have to pay your way in to hear it. Civility and courtesy are not protected by the Constitution, even if, as I always understood it, when you bought a ticket, you were, in effect, buying a license that could be revoked.

At least the assistant attorney general of Maryland has concluded that offensive speech in a public place is not an unalloyed right, especially when exercised before what he calls "captive auditors." I understand that "captive auditors" means, in particular, children. But it is a phrase I am proud to embrace for myself. From now on, in whatever public space, or wherever in the presence of cell phones, I will think of myself as a captive auditor. It is good to have a fancy official name for being a victim.

From both an auditory and visual position, though, the single worst word that has ever been unleashed on sports is "sucks." It is not a dirty word; I can say it on the radio, as I just did. But it is such a rude, nasty little word, isn't it? Frankly, there are a lot of dirty words I like better. But fans love to scream, ad nauseam, that the opponents suck or such-and-such a player sucks. In the fashion of the times, they even chant it. Or they print the same things on T-shirts, and people actually think it makes them really clever fans if they walk around in T-shirts that say "So-and-So Sucks." If I could ask one thing of the Neanderthal creeps at games who bother captive auditors like me, it would be to at least come up with another rude and childish word to replace "sucks."

And thank you, also, for standing on the right and walking on the left.

Past-ism

2013

The Great Gatsby is on the screen again, reopening the perennial debate about whether or not it is the great American novel. Or was that *Adventures of Huckleberry Finn*? Or are we still waiting for the great American novel? Is the title vacant, like most recent Tour de France championships? In the arts, the argument over the great American novel is a rather unusual great fuss about the greatest. In most disciplines there simply doesn't seem to be a passion to constantly assess who's number one. Except, except . . .

In sport, it's imperative not only to decide who is the greatest, but also to regularly find the latest greatest in sport. All this comes to mind now because there's a groundswell to ordain LeBron James as the greatest basketball player ever. Poor Michael Jordan, he barely had time for a quick cup of coffee at the top of the historical tree.

Unlike in art or music or drama, this manic determination in sport to promote someone new is prompted by the fact that whereas we can't statistically compare, say, Beethoven and Mozart, sports provide simple benchmarks. Usain Bolt runs the one hundred meter faster than did that old slowpoke Carl Lewis, and much faster than the turtle-like Jesse Owens, ergo not only is Bolt thereby demonstratively the greatest, it also means that his twenty-first-century contemporaries in team sports—similarly bigger and stronger and faster—must likewise be better in their games than all who came before.

Indeed, to many fans—especially the younger ones—there's a prejudice in sport that might be called past-ism. It's laughable to these modern critics that anyone from yore can be taken seriously in comparison with today's modern marvels. Numbers prove everything! Jim Brown and Bobby Orr and Rod Laver and Jerry West and Bobby Jones would be merely serviceable role players in the company of today's advanced human specimens.

The great irony, though, is that with the possible exception of music, nothing makes us more nostalgic than sport. We *adore* the sporting past. Why, Mr. Fitzgerald could've been talking strictly about sports when he famously concluded: "So we beat on, boats against the current, borne back ceaselessly into the past."

But, paradoxically, as much as we gloriously revel in what was past in sport, we always make sure then to ceaselessly denigrate those golden days as merely quaint, a lesser thing than what nature's superior athletic paragons give us today.

Let's Give 'Em a Hand

2010

It occurred to my friend the Duchess, the sports connoisseur who seeks out all that may be indecorous in athletics, that there is a glaring lapse of etiquette in one sport.

Writing to me from her yacht, as always, in her lovely cursive hand, she begins: "If I am not mistaken, my dear Frank, among major sports, baseball players are the only ones who never shake hands with each other in the spirit of goodwill. What a dreadfully rude lapse of manners."

The Duchess went on to note that basketball players are the most social. The starters shake hands before the game and often kibitz on the court afterward. Moreover, after college games, the two teams all pass by each other in a line, sort of like a Virginia reel at a square dance.

Even those whom the Duchess called "ruffians on ice" may pound each other all season, but when a hockey playoff series is over and one team is eliminated, the players on both teams, including the goons, skate slowly past each other and shake hands.

As the Duchess wrote: "I find that really quite lovely, Frank. Even brutes can be taught to be civilized upon occasion."

Further, the Duchess pointed out that football players mingle on the field after every game, as she wrote, "rather as their fans tailgate."

The "concussion candidates," as the Duchess labeled football players, tend to mate up by position. Always, the quarterback from one team seeks out the quarterback from the other. The coaches at least acknowledge one another even if they can't stand each other, and the more religious players from both teams even join together in a circle and pray.

Golfers make sure to shake hands with the other players' caddies. "Very egalitarian, don't you think, Frank?" Yes, indeed, Duchess.

And tennis players meet at the net. It used to be that the winner might jump the net, but there's a certain triumphalism to that, so the custom's pretty much gone out.

The last man the Duchess could remember jumping the net was Bobby Riggs, after Billie Jean King creamed him. "A gallant display of testosterone," the Duchess suggested. Boxers, of course, touch gloves before the fight after the referee opines, "May the best man win." And my gracious, exclaimed the Duchess, soccer players and rowers, even literally, give each other the shirts off their backs.

The Duchess concluded her letter to me, noting how especially curious it was, that while baseball players do not congratulate each other after the game, they're quite convivial during the game. If a batter hits a double, he'll be sure to pass the time with the opposition shortstop or second baseman.

Afterward, though, it's only the winners who come out on the field and fist bump each other.

"I wish the losers would at least tip their hats to their conquerors," the Duchess concluded. "There is no reason why baseball players can't be gentlemen, like others of the sporting persuasion."

Southern Comfort

2012

Well, the Southeastern Conference season has begun. I have it on good authority that other college football teams around the country will also be playing games this fall.

I don't know when exactly the SEC took over America. I know this is hard to believe, but the epicenter of college football used to be in the Midwest. I'm so old, I can remember when Notre Dame actually mattered, and the real tough players were supposed to come from western Pennsylvania and Ohio.

Now, this is not to say that college football in the South hasn't always been important. Football is the war game, and Dixie has always produced a disproportionate number of our warriors. Major-league professional sports were late in coming to the South, so college football down there has, even now, less competition.

But the national primacy of the SEC is relatively new. SEC teams have won the past six Bowl Championship Series titles, and the SEC has not only a huge, multibillion-dollar contract with ESPN, but also a backup one with CBS, so both networks swoon over the SEC. The national hype now exists alongside the regional passion. The SEC is ubiquitous.

And it's also expanding. The SEC has moved out into Texas and up into Missouri. Basically, though, the SEC has always been Deep South, plus Kentucky. Kentucky is apparently allowed in the conference so that everybody else but Vanderbilt gets a guaranteed win—plus, Kentucky bourbon can fuel those famous southern tailgate parties.

But, of course, it's impossible to ignore the pride the South feels for its football. As no other section of the country remains so closely connected—"Save your Confederate money, boys!"—so does no other section of the country boast of a regional predominance in any sport. Just because the Yankees have won all these years, the Northeast has never said, "Hey, we got the best baseball up here."

It's impossible not to sense that because the South usually brings up the rear in important things like health, education, and income, it looks to college football to enhance its national standing. We're number one, well, in something else besides beauty pageants. In the new book *Better Off Without 'Em*, in which the author, Chuck Thompson, argues that the rest of the country would be improved if the South really did secede, he quotes Colin Cowherd, an ESPN host, as accounting for the SEC's success primarily because the region is so high in "poverty and obesity." The South's pride in its college football success is really quite analogous to what Notre Dame used to mean to Roman Catholics back when there was tremendous prejudice against their religion, and its parishioners were viewed as second-class citizens.

But what is different today is that southerners are not just loyal to their particular football school. The team's league has earned an allegiance that truly matters and is unique in American sport. Of course, it also helps, as always, that the SEC is a winner.

ELEVEN

Artful

2007

Sport is not considered art. Instead, it is invariably dismissed as something lesser—even something rather more vulgar—than the more traditional performance activities.

Well, apart from simply being so sweaty, I think sport has suffered in comparison with the arts—or I might be so bold as to say: the *other* arts—because it is founded on trying to win. Artists are not supposed to be competitive. They're expected to be above that. We always hear "art for art's sake." Nobody ever says "sport for sport's sake."

I also believe that sport has suffered because, until recently, athletic performance could not be preserved. What we accepted as great art—whether the book, the painting, the sculpture, the symphony—is that which could be saved and savored. But the performances of the athletic artists who ran and jumped and wrestled were gone with the wind. We are all familiar with the famous Greek statue of the discus thrower, but forgotten is who he was, what he achieved in his performance as an athlete.

Now, however, we can study the grace of the athlete on film. A double play can be viewed as pretty as a pas de deux, a Roger Federer backhand seen as lovely as a Monet water lily. Is not what we saw Michael Jordan do every bit as artistic as what we saw Mikhail Baryshnikov do?

Of course, in the academic world, precisely that place where art is defined and certified, sport is its own worst enemy. Its corruption in college diminishes it so and makes it all seem so grubby. But just because so many ersatz students are shoe-horned into colleges as athletes and then kept eligible academically through various deceits, the intrinsic essence of the athlete playing his game should not be affected.

As Gary Walters, the athletic director at Princeton, says: "Athletic competition nourishes our collective souls and contributes to the holistic education of the total person in the same manner as the arts."

Certainly, there remains a huge double standard in college. Why can a young musician major in music, a young actor major in drama, but a young football player can't major in football? That not only strikes me as unfair; it encourages the situation where those hidebound defenders of the artistic faith can take delight in looking down their noses at sport.

But it is only a fine line between the touch of a winning jump shot at the buzzer and the sensitivity of an actress looking for the kindness of strangers. Or, just because you can bet on something, does that disqualify it as a thing of beauty?

Gone Fishin'

1997

In Colorado last week I watched two men happily fishing in a mountain stream. A few days later, right in Central Park, in the wilds of Manhattan, I paused as a father showed his young son how to cast. At a cocktail party not long ago, I was corralled by a couple wanting to know if I'd seen a wonderful new book, featuring pictures of . . . trout. And all year, at varying times, friends of mine depart the ease of civilization to go somewhere primitive, where, for the privilege of being cold and uncomfortable, they can . . . fish.

And the thing that confounds me most—even more than the choosing to be uncomfortable part—is that while I know golfers I cannot tolerate and tennis players I can't abide, I've never met a fisherman I didn't like . . . well, so long as he didn't try to talk to me about fishing.

So I am, all in all, very jealous of fishermen. They must have some secret. Even two thousand years ago, Jesus obviously knew what he was up to when he, a carpenter, picked so many fishermen for his disciples. After all, it isn't just me. Nobody dislikes fishermen. We may not understand them. We may not have a clue why they do to themselves what they choose to do—but we certainly don't harbor any antipathy toward them.

It's ironic, too. A lot of people loathe hunters. Why, in England now, the most pressing national issue concerns foxhunters. Never mind Princess Di's new beau, the country is torn about whether to outlaw men in Pink coats chasing foxes.

But ban their alter egos in high rubber boots seeking after rainbow trout? When you think about it, what's the difference between bringing Bambi down with a rifle slug and hauling in some handsome walleyed pike with a mean hook? It isn't that fish are any less deserving than others of God's creatures. Why, it is certified that salmon know geography better than 92 percent of American high school students, and dolphins are not only cute as buttons, but are smarter than all talk-show hosts and most football players.

So why don't we get more exercised about killing our marine friends?

Not only that, but when fishermen prey on these dear little creatures of the deep, they use . . . what? Right. They use *lures*. Dirty pool.

Moreover, when it comes to fishermen, it is simply assumed that they are liars. They will not tell the simple truth about the ones that got away. Nonetheless, we blithely accept prevarication when it comes to our fishing brethren. Nobody, you see, ever wants to say anything bad about fishermen. Why doesn't somebody tell Newt Gingrich to go fish? That is the way to popularity. In fact, the last president who was a genuine fisherman was Dwight Eisenhower, and Ike was the most beloved president. It figures.

But, you see, I don't think you can pretend to like fishing. I think the sport sorts out the ones who would fish for show, for style, for the wrong reasons. Years ago, I was down in Oklahoma with a wry old basketball coach named Abe Lemons.

Since he was the quintessential country boy, I just assumed he fished. So I asked him about it.

"Fish?" Abe groaned. "Son, I don't like myself that much."

Maybe that's it. Maybe that's why, much as I'd like it, I never can hang that sign on my door that says: "GONE FISHIN'!"

Nouveau Heart and Mind

2012

Jacques Barzun, the esteemed cultural historian, lived 104 years and wrote a multitude of words about the most important issues in society, but when he died last week, his one quote that was invariably cited was a pithy one that he wrote back in 1954: "Whoever wants to know the heart and mind of America had better learn baseball."

Never mind that that is no longer even remotely true.

For, yes, as the World Series had among its lowest television ratings ever, it was even more evident that football is now far and away our national game. Baseball was the national pastime, but nobody would dare call football a pantywaist thing like "pastime." Football means business.

Of course, all sorts of treatises have been written comparing the two sports, but none has been so brilliant as the comic routine that the late George Carlin developed, in which he described baseball as a "nineteenth-century pastoral game" and football as a "twentieth-century technological struggle." He went on to contrast the two, using a harsh, gruff voice for the gridiron—"in football you wear a helmet"—and a sweet, near-falsetto for the diamond: "in baseball you wear a cap."

But Mr. Barzun's death, which obliquely served to turn his famous old observation into an epitaph for baseball's pre-eminence, does make us wonder why football has supplanted baseball so in popularity. Does it tell us anything about ourselves? Or as Mary McGrory, the late Pulitzer Prize–winning columnist, framed it most succinctly back when football was ascending: "Baseball is what we were. Football is what we have become."

So, do we love football more because the essence of football is brutality, and we are now a more violent people? Or does the fact that football is easier to bet on account for our greater fondness for it? Or maybe, above all, is it simply that football eclipsed baseball because it is so perfect for television?

It is ironic, too, that even as women have become so much more involved in sports, football is the one retrograde game which is played almost exclusively by boys and men. Might football not be that twenty-first-century technological struggle after all, but instead, at heart, a subversive vestige of the male-centric past?

Whatever, indisputably, football remains uniquely our game, even as so much else in the cultural world—music, movies, video, video games, fashion, and most sports, too—catches on all over the world. However, except perhaps across the border with our Canadian cousins, no one else plays what is knowingly dismissed as American football.

Talk about United States exceptionalism in this America-first election year. Baseball is still an extremely popular entertainment, but whoever wants to know the taste and passion of America had better learn football.

Little Big Man

2003

My mother always told me it was rude to stare, but I remember the first time I saw Bill Shoemaker. I couldn't take my eyes off him. It was not because I was a kid in awe at this great jockey. Rather it was just how perfect he fit together. The Shoe was dressed nattily, sitting at the bar sipping a martini after an afternoon of race riding at Hialeah.

What struck me so was the proportion of the man. He might have only been four feet eleven and maybe one hundred pounds, but everything about him was just right; balanced, only downsized. He was the best-looking hors d'oeuvre of a man I ever saw.

Maybe that's why Shoemaker could surely sit a horse as well as anyone who was ever boosted up into a saddle. He did not seem to move. We've heard of poetry in motion. Bill Shoemaker was poetry at rest. Indeed, in his early riding days at Midcentury in Northern California, the stewards thought the bug boy—what apprentices are called—was not trying. They wanted to ground him. Why, he never even seemed to bother with the whip.

But there was this problem. Shoemaker's mounts kept winning, even if they crossed the finish line with him sitting still, their ears pricked up as if they were out for a morning canter. An old trainer once said it best. "Shoe rides a horse like it was a swan."

Shoemaker's other great asset was his hands. A horse could sense the little man's assuredness from his steady rump, then know when to move at the tender touch of his fingers on the reins. So the Shoe, whose shoe size, by the way, was two and a half, rode forty thousand mounts over four decades, winning 8,800 races.

Ironically, of all that he did win, one race that he lost when he was young still stands out. In the 1957 Kentucky Derby on Gallant Man, he thought the race ended at the sixteenth pole and stood up in the irons for an instant before he realized his mistake. It cost Shoemaker the roses.

Curiously, too, the Shoe's most famous victory came when he was fifty-four, well past his prime. But he stole Ferdinand through a hole at the top of the stretch and rode him home for his fourth Derby. That was in 1986. In 1991, less than a year after he retired, Shoemaker was paralyzed in an automobile accident. The athlete who had such an exquisite touch would live out his life without sensation. The hands, those wonderful, tiny hands, lay forever limp by his side.

Just a few months ago Shoemaker heard the news that Ferdinand had died in Japan in a slaughterhouse, sold for horse meat. Now the jock, a quadriplegic, is gone too. He hit the finish line, as they would say at the track, in seventy-two years and change. No one ever lived sitting so pretty.

Life in the
Time of Drugs

2004

It's easiest to conclude, of course, that athletes will do just about anything to win. Each advance in training that was originally frowned upon only eventually came to be accepted. Professionalism was not sporting. Neither was hiring a coach. Athletic scholarships were unlawful. Don't lift weights. And on and on. Who's to say we won't someday accept steroids as just another training device, nothing more than a better pair of Nikes?

But then it's also just as true that many athletes will do anything for money, or for the vanity, for hanging onto the good life of a hero. Who knows all the complex motives that have inspired athletes to risk their reputations and their health by taking illegal drugs?

And, of course, it's probably easier to cheat this way nowadays, because modern athletes have grown up comfortably in an environment where drugs are an accepted part of everyday life. There's no stigma attached to taking drugs now—especially in our impatient world where instant gratification rules. If drugs are accepted everywhere else, how do you draw the line at games? Hey, the most prominent commercials on sports TV used to be the big three beers: Budweiser, Miller, and Coors.

Now the big three seem to be Viagra, Levitra, and Cialis. What's a little anabolic steroid, a touch of human growth hormone, among friends?

Ah, but perhaps more than anything, Ponce de León remains with us all. Yes, some young world-class Olympic champions have succumbed to the temptation of drugs, but it is the aging athlete who is most susceptible to the charms of steroids. Just give me a few more seasons in the sun. Don't let it end now . . . not yet. Please, God, please. Sebastian Coe, the great British miler, said once, "Suddenly, I got to the age of thirty-six and one day I realized: I can't ever run any quicker than I'm running at this moment. And that's when the candle didn't flicker—it went out." Coe came to that stark realization in the middle of a workout. He stopped dead right there and never ran another step.

But that's not normal. Most athletes would do anything to hold back the night, to buy just a little more time. Anything, just to keep on being thirty-six for a few more years. Hey, it's no different from older actresses getting breast implants to keep up with the ingenues, is it?

The irony with Jason Giambi and Barry Bonds and the other obvious suspects, though, is that the drugs have become too good. They didn't just keep their careers going a while longer, magically preserving their youth for another summer or two. The drugs made their counterfeit selves even better than what nature had given them in the very glory of their pretty youth. So they got carried away with their own artificiality and flew too close to the sun. Poor devils—they had come to believe that their wings were real.

GMs and ADs

2014

One great mystery of sport is why they call the place that the general manager rules over "the Front Office." Obviously, it's the box office that's out front. What they call the Front Office is really the Office-Office.

College sports never had a Front Office. It sounds too commercial, too unacademic. So it's called the Athletic Department, pretending to be like the Geology Department or the Romance Languages Department—if there're any of them left.

Anyway, the Front Office has grown exponentially. Once it was pretty much just the general manager himself, who was known cutely as the "GM." Then they added scouts. Now there are many *assistant* GMs, who I know not what they do. Because also ensconced in the Front Office are powerful sorcerers, known as statisticians, who tell the general manager that their numbers *prove* which players are really good, notwithstanding what the expensive genius general manager thinks he sees with his own educated eyes.

Another change is that the general managers now usually have the title of president. Uh-oh. Once general managers started to be called presidents, the law of unintended consequences set in, and that made an owner think that in order to one-up his president, he had to do more than just own. And that screwed up Front Office even more.

Coaches get famous, but as a general rule, coaches don't make good general managers. Different talents. It's the same as how the best assistant coaches usually don't make good head coaches. Different talents. In a more innocent time, college athletic directors—ADs—were usually just worn-out old football coaches kicked upstairs for their golden years. There were no women's sports then or other nuisances to bother with. It is instructive that the athletic director who changed college sports, really made them mercantile, was a track coach at Michigan back in the seventies named Don Canham, who got sick of coaching track. Wouldn't you? Don Canham was the operator who thought athletic departments could be Walmarts, with teams on the side. Very savvy guy.

About the worst sports franchise is the New York Knicks, where the meddlesome birdbrain owner has hired the brilliant coach Phil Jackson to be general manager—oh, excuse me, to be president. What made Jackson so successful was that he could relate to his players, actually *coach* them. He had a shtick that was hyped as sort of trickle-down Zen. However, these talents are pretty useless in the Front Office. Jackson will surely get a disciple to coach the team. Everybody will say Jackson has *installed* so-and-so as his coach, which sounds to the players like they just put in a new washing machine. It never works.

If I were an owner, I would hire a general manager to be general manager and I would *call* him general manager. And then I would stay out of the Front Office.

End of a Love Affair

2012

Individual sports are always volatile, and after being the next big thing, NASCAR's popularity has stalled.

Yes, a lot simply had to do with the economy. In a sport that depends on sponsorships and rich owners—like those good buddies Mitt Romney kicks tires with—NASCAR was especially vulnerable.

And as for fans, when it became cutback time, they had to think twice about gassing up those big old RVs and driving a far piece to sit in those ear-shattering stadiums.

So, NASCAR invested $5 million in research to find out how to get back out of the pits. To me, the most fascinating finding was that all those old, white guys, who were the bread-and-butter NASCAR constituency, were not being replenished by their sons and grandsons. Frankly, the younger generations don't care to mess around with cars.

Ladies and gentlemen, I know this is heresy. It's been a given that Americans have what is always called "a love affair with the car." But what NASCAR found out was that it's now only a platonic relationship. No hands on. A whole cohort of our young boys—and girls—has been growing up without any interest in messing around—tinkering—with cars. It made me think that the last time I ever heard anybody talking about looking under the hood was when Ross Perot ran for president in '92, and he kept saying all we had to do to fix things was look under the hood.

Well, NASCAR found, nobody much wants to do that anymore. Sure, younger people still view automobiles as a necessary evil to get from point A to B, but no less so than do Brazilians or Indians or the Chinese.

In fact, Americans aren't satisfied only to drive. They otherwise want to talk on the phone, eat and drink, text, plug in their iPods, fool around with the GPS, or—the best and brightest of them—listen to NPR. How many Americans would even get into cars if they couldn't be entertained while driving?

It's not just cars, either. Whereas races were always the mainstay of sport, going back to Paleolithic times, simple speed is itself out of fashion. Horse racing lost its place at the top tier of American sports as soon as other forms of gambling were legalized, and people racing—the track in track and field—is not nearly as popular as it once was.

Speed records used to be so stylish—horses, human beings, cars, planes, boats. Remember the regular Bonneville Flats hullabaloo? Now that's ho-hum. *The Amazing Race*, on television, is probably our most popular race now, precisely because it's not a race, but a game first, full of fun obstacles.

Not only that, but when it comes to cars, kids grow up being primarily accustomed to watching cars crashing in movies and on TV. Cars going fast? What's sexy about cars now is that they're instruments of demolition.

And tinker? Researchers at the University of Michigan found that the kids who tinker more with the Internet delay getting their driver's licenses. Not wanting a driver's license? Next to making out, that was *the* most important rite of passage in an American teenager's life.

Look, I wish NASCAR well. I hope it gets people back to the races, but it is going to have to do it with stars and steroids and point spreads, like all the other sports. Nobody cool wants to look under the hood anymore. They want to look at Facebook and YouTube. I can officially declare that, as of 2012, the American love affair with the car is over. Cars are so Greatest Generation.

TWELVE

Presidential
Exploitation

2011

Next week, at some place in Indianapolis, where time has been instructed to stand still, Mark Emmert, president of the NCAA, will convene what is being called, without irony, a "retreat." Assembled will be about fifty college presidents, pledged, it seems, to make sure that college athletics continue to remain firmly in the past, in the antiquated amateur hours.

The avowed purpose of cloistering the academic intelligentsia is about "protecting and enhancing the integrity of intercollegiate athletics," which is the equivalent, say, of upholding the gold standard of the government of Somalia. Will there be just one president among the two score and ten with the courage to suggest that the empire has no wardrobe, that it just doesn't work anymore?

Emmert should certainly know. Both colleges whose presidential mansions he graced, Louisiana State University and the University of Washington, have been punished by the NCAA. But, of course, many of the presidents will be coming from athletically convicted campuses. It's certainly worth highlighting that the two prime incumbent NCAA champions, Auburn in football, University of Connecticut in basketball, are both current offenders—UConn convicted, Auburn, already a serial cheat, under investigation again. If that suggests to you that virtue may be its own reward but see-no-evil is the path to trophy, well then, you are college presidential timber.

If the retreat would only admit that the reason integrity has flown the coop is because it is impossible for billion-dollar entertainment industries—which is what ticket sales, concessions, and TV contracts make college football and basketball to be—to logically exist when everybody is making money but the entertainers themselves. Never mind fairness; it is against human nature. The system obliges hypocrisy and mandates deceit.

Yet a stated purpose of the retreat is to "maintain amateurism"—even as more and more observers and insiders, including coaches, have changed their minds and concluded that the NCAA must acknowledge that the nineteenth century really did end sometime ago.

The NCAA claims that amateurism equates to purity. That is a canard; there is simply no proof of that. Otherwise we would have amateur musicians, painters, and writers, and art would flourish pristine as never before.

The NCAA's stated defense for athletic penury is "student-athletes should be protected from exploitation." Hear! Hear! But right now, it's the NCAA member colleges that exploit football and basketball players.

Would there be just one president at the retreat who would speak the truth and acknowledge that the only true reason for amateurism in big-time college sports is because it allows colleges to get something for free with which to amuse the paying students and fleece the wealthy alumni?

Wistful Day

2004

Yesterday was our day to be thankful. I think perhaps we also ought to have one designated day set aside every year to be wistful, to remember, fondly, the things we don't have anymore. So, for this first Wistful Day, in sports, I wish we still had:

- The Statue of Liberty play in football.
- Short pants in basketball.
- And baseball caps that are worn the right way, brim facing forward.
- The *Gillette Friday Night Fights* commercial that had a parrot—don't ask why—that said: "Look sharp, feel sharp."
- I wish we still had Joe Garagiola doing the Westminster Dog Show.
- Sunday baseball double-headers that only cost one ticket.
- The Roller Derby, especially the saintly Joanie Weston popping the villainous Anne Calvello.
- One heavyweight champion. One light-heavyweight champion. One middleweight champion . . . you get the idea.

- The Southwest Conference.
- I wish we still had hockey players skating without helmets, so you could see their faces well, even if they didn't have any teeth.
- Baseball announcers and writers who were not embarrassed to say "twin killing" when they meant a double play and "round tripper" when they meant a home run.
- Cheerleaders leading a cheer that went: "Sampson, Sampson, he's our man. / If he can't do it, no one can."
- Jai alai: it was so exotic. Whatever happened to jai alai?
- I wish we still had golf tournaments that were played without idiots screaming, "You da man."
- Pitchers who threw complete games.
- Tennis players who could serve and volley.
- Teams that were called "varsities" instead of "programs." I also always especially liked junior varsities. Jayvees. That's such an evocative word—jayvee. Does anybody even care about jayvees anymore?
- I wish they still had creative nicknames for players, and didn't just call guys by their numbers or initials. What kind of a nickname was M.J.? I think the last good name was the Refrigerator.
- The Quebec Nordiques, the Los Angeles Rams, the Baltimore Colts, the Hartford Whalers, and possibly the entire American Basketball Association. Anyway, the ABA's red-white-and-blue ball.
- Stealing home. Has anybody even tried to steal home since Jackie Robinson?
- Country-boy players who hunted and fished in the off-season.
- I wish they still called basketball players "cagers."

- Earl Weaver, Lefty Driesell, Arnold Palmer, and Smarty Jones.
- The mile instead of the fifteen hundred meters.
- End zones that just had slanted vertical stripes. Oh, those were the days. And . . .
- The Curse of the Bambino.

Miss that already, don't you?

Fat Chance

2001

I remember when I was a boy the day after Christmas was always devoted to testing presents. Even if the weather was cold, if I'd gotten some athletic equipment, it was requisite to go outside and try it out. Ooh, did it sting when your father or your buddy tossed you a ball into your shiny new baseball mitt. I know that time and technology march on, and I'm not foolishly reminiscing about a return to the halcyon days of marbles and mumblety-peg, but I do wonder how many kids get holiday sports presents this year as opposed to all those electronic games.

The fact remains that as even the most recent government report so dramatically showed us, our children, not unlike the rest of us, are getting fatter. When American kids play, more and more they do it while sitting on their bottoms, not standing, let alone running, on their legs. And as we sit, usually to watch television, so do we eat too much, too. Especially when I return from a trip abroad, I'm always astounded at the size of the portions on our dinner plates.

There is specifically some immutable law that the number of french fries served must grow exponentially every year. French fries on American plates appear to breed like guinea pigs. Our mid-twentieth-century dominion over sports was bound to diminish as the rest of the world became healthier and wealthier and wise to coaching, but it's obvious that now we don't even produce athletes commensurate with our numbers, our power, and our wealth. Our middle-class white boys— smiling, wholesome crew cuts who used to grow up to be our all-American heroes—have basically disappeared. African Americans dominate basketball and football, two of our most popular team sports, and more and more Hispanics command the other, baseball.

Basically whites, those who constitute our numerical majority and who are our most advantaged, only manage to be competitive with their arms as baseball pitchers and football quarterbacks. The most international of individual sports, tennis, is particularly illuminating as a symbol of American athletic decline. A generation ago, half the best tennis players, male and female, were from the United States, but now only perhaps a fifth of the top women and less than a tenth of the men are American.

It's instructive that movies and television most try and attract that young, white, and affluent audience, and television is doing a fine job. Our children are growing up as very good watchers but, it appears, not very aggressive doers. Thank heaven for golf, a sport which the *New England Journal of Medicine* says has the exercise coefficient of gardening. Golf seems to be the perfect sport for our sedentary nation. As a double minority of Asian and African heritage, Tiger Woods was something of a novelty on the links, especially succeeding as he did at such a young age. But now a seventeen-year-old suburban white lad, one Ty Tyron, has won a place on the PGA Tour and we can only assume that more and more of our young Lochinvars will be surrendering team games and more strenuous individual sports to hop into their carts and fire off down the fairway.

No, it's not a crisis, but you do have to wonder about a nation whose young are so fat and happy and whether or not their inability to be competitive in sports will eventually be reflected in other, more important life endeavors.

Game Changer

2012

We're all familiar with the many sports terms that have moved into general usage: "par for the course," "slam dunk," "curveball," "photo finish," and so on. Curiously, though, every now and then something of the inverse occurs, and we get an expression which is commonly used that has been derived from sport, but never used in sport.

For example, that awful, overdone cliché, "level playing field." Never in my life have I ever heard anyone in sport—that is, somebody actually right there on the level playing field—say: "I'm glad we're playing on a level playing field."

Likewise: "The ball is in your court." Nobody in tennis ever says that. Among other things, by the time you did say it, the ball would already be back over the net—right smack in your own court.

Or: "soccer moms." Does any mother who has a child on a soccer team ever call herself a soccer mom? No. And by the way, whatever happened to the word "mother"? Nobody ever says "mother" anymore. Everybody just says "mom." When I was growing up, I had a mom, and my buddy had a mom—but if you referred to more than one mom, you always said "mothers." There were no "working moms" then, or "Gold

Star Moms," or "moms of invention," and certainly no "soccer moms."

But now we have a very popular new sports term that is never used in sports: "game changer." Where did that come from? Nobody who plays a game ever says the game had a game changer. No, it has forever been obligatory in sport to say "turning point." Real games have turning points. But things that are not games have game changers.

Here, though, is a game changer, uniformwise, that especially interests me. The star rookie quarterback of the Washington Redskins is named Robert Lee Griffin III. And so far as I know, he is the first player ever—ever—in the entire history of sports uniforms, to have "the third" on his uniform. It says "GRIFFIN III."

You see, this especially interests me because I happen to be a third myself, although I dropped it as soon as my grandfather died and there weren't three of us with the same name around anymore. I don't know about young Mr. Griffin, but it's a terrible thing being the third. There's no place to put Roman numerals on forms. And it sounds snooty, like you're an earl or a duke, and sometimes you get mail addressed to Mr. Iii. However, maybe if you have "the third" on the back of your uniform, this problem will not develop.

In any event, I am sure that all the other American thirds, like me, are rooting for Robert Lee Griffin III. I hope his jersey is a big seller—so us thirds will finally come into fashion.

There's No "I" in U.S.A.

2011

I've always thought that one of the best things about American sports is that we aren't dominated by one team game, as so much of the rest of the world is soccercentric. That's why we can have our own American dream. The dream of most other countries is simply to have their national soccer team do well.

We spread around our devotion to all sorts of different teams: baseball and softball, football, basketball, ice hockey, soccer—professional teams, college teams, even high school teams. Yes, Americans are much more serial team fans than those in other nations, who tend to be more monogamous in their sporting affection.

However, the downside of this focus on team sports is becoming apparent. The United States is less and less a power in some individual sports—especially the old country-club games of golf and tennis.

For the first time ever, the four men's major golf titles are held by foreigners, all members of the European tour. Except for the Williams sisters, no American, male or female, has won one of the Grand Slam tennis championships in the past seven years—and right now, it looks like another biblical seven years of tennis famine lies ahead here. We do somewhat better in women's golf, but still, it's been seventeen years since an American woman, Betsy King, finished number one on the LPGA tour.

Now, obviously, part of the reason for this depressing situation is that the rest of the world has caught up with us in sports as sure as it has in many other respects.

But I also think that because we concentrate so on team sports, from a very early age, in schools, American athletes tend to find a team game that appeals to them. On the other hand, a good young foreign athlete who doesn't much like soccer is more inclined to try an individual sport instead. As a consequence, most of our good tennis players and golfers don't stumble into those sports through public programs, as players do in foreign countries, but take to them only because of family influence.

Much is made of the fact that Venus and Serena Williams and Tiger Woods are rare African American stars in their sports, but the more salient fact is that all three were taught their sports by their fathers, just like so many of our best white players. Their race is merely incidental, for their path to the top is typically American.

I'm especially surprised that more of the best American girl athletes don't try tennis, because for females it's such a high-profile sport, with much more potential for fame and fortune. Maria Sharapova is richer and better known than any American woman playing basketball, softball, or soccer. Can't anybody figure that out but Richard Williams, Venus and Serena's father?

The cliché is that there's no "I" in team. But more and more, when it comes to tennis and golf, there's no "U.S." in world champion.

Gimme That Old-Time Momentum

1999

I know I'm just getting started in this commentary, but please give me a chance to build up a little momentum. This goes for you, too, in your daily lives. You've got to have momentum.

Momentum is especially important in football, though, even if I'm not quite sure what exactly it is. It's been around for a long time, too. Why, it even used to be called "Big Mo." But now momentum is too important to be treated with such familiarity. As football announcers forever tell us, if a team has momentum, that is good. If it doesn't, well then, a team must go get momentum.

As nearly as I can tell, momentum is like oxygen or advertising or bad taste. It is always there. I know this because momentum shifts. The announcers advise us of that with great gravity. "Well, it looks like the momentum has shifted." First one team has it, you see—then the other. Nobody ever says: "What's completely missing today is momentum."

No, the first law of football momentum is that there is always momentum, and the announcers are never more downcast than when a team loses its momentum. The tone then is forlorn, spoken in the same manner as when Peter Pan lost his shadow or Eeyore his tail.

I always try to maintain my composure during these instances, because I know that either (a) momentum will be regained or (b) momentum will shift. It always does one or the other. If it's football, there simply must be momentum. Somewhere out there.

Momentum is not rife in other games. It's never in baseball. I'm not so sure about hockey. In basketball, yes, there is momentum, but most times, instead of having momentum a team is described as "on a run." I don't think that's quite the same thing.

Well, what do you think? Have I built up enough momentum yet in this commentary?

Actually, the other time when we are told there is a lot of momentum is a primary election campaign. A candidate will win a couple primaries, and the pundits will then say that the other candidates have to "stop his momentum."

This is where football and politics are different, momentumwise. In football, the announcers never suggest that the team that has momentum can have it wrested away. No, momentum belongs to you. It's entirely up to you whether you will keep it or not.

The thing about momentum in football is that it is all-embracing. I used to think that momentum was, well, in layman's terms, sort of the opposite of inertia. But now, momentum has been expanded to the point where it represents "good." If you are playing well, you have momentum. If you are not playing well, you don't have momentum. You have to find some momentum.

And now, while this commentary has run out of momentum, I hope that you and yours have it tightly in your grasp.

Mulligans

2013

When my old pal the Sports Curmudgeon had some mildly churlish things to say about golf a few weeks ago, both he and I were upbraided by loyal linksters. As one snapped at me: "You don't know anything about golf." Perhaps.

But I do know all about golf propaganda.

Because major golf tournaments continue to maintain a nineteenth-century pose and require golfers to keep their own score, instead of having a paid scorekeeper with a twenty-first-century electronic device—as is the case with every other big-time sport—golfers love to pretend that this somehow makes the sport more noble. The tiresome network shills can never stop boasting about how golf is a more honorable game than all the others.

But really, that's just silly. Is there anything more archaic than requiring the golfers—after a round that has dragged on for several hours, with every shot dutifully recorded on TV—to repair to some secret rendezvous where, I believe, there is an abacus, to make sure everybody can count to seventy-one? Then they sign their scorecards like they were the Declaration of Independence. Imagine: Sign here, Mr. LeBron James, to certify that you really did make the thirty-six points we all saw you score on network television.

The primary contention that golfers alone keep their own scores is, itself, a myth. Go to any club or public park and watch the tennis players, the handball players, the guys playing basketball. They all keep their own score. Just like golfers. And for that matter, you don't think it's more ethically challenging calling a cross-court shot your tennis opponent slugged into the corner than hitting your own stationary ball sitting there still on a tee?

The only difference between golf and every other sport is that golf alone ludicrously persists in having its *professionals* play by the same antiquated rules as weekend duffers. Oh, I've got a good idea! Let's get rid of linesmen and have Novak Djokovic and Andy Murray keep their own score at Wimbledon, to prove how honorable they are.

And, just for the record, no sport is more associated with gambling than golf is. Gambling is part of the human condition—no big deal. But it's also the case that where people bet, there's a greater temptation to cheat. Golf is the sport for the athletic angels among us? Please.

Look, golf may be a fine game. But nothing is more irritating than to hear this con that its players are pure and chivalrous while all other athletes are immoral scoundrels. Cut the PR folderol. I guarantee you that Diogenes didn't put away his lantern when he first stumbled onto a golf course.

THIRTEEN

The Other State U's

2002

I've always had a soft spot in my heart for the teams at the State U's. You know, those schools that are *not* the "University of" something, like the University of Michigan or the University of Virginia, but have the word "state" in their title, like Oregon State or Mississippi State.

State colleges invariably were created after the "University of" colleges. Usually, the "University of" colleges are the more hoity-toity places. They like to call themselves the "flagships." Oooh. By contrast, a lot of state colleges started out as agricultural schools—"aggies," like marbles—so stuck-up fans of the aristocratic university schools would all go "Mooo" during games, and holler other nasty barnyard things.

Or, in the South, the state colleges were the predominantly black schools, like Tennessee State and Kentucky State. Or they started out as teachers colleges, or, heaven forbid, even as colleges for young ladies, like Florida State.

Whatever the original reason, schools with "state" in their name invariably never have the cachet that the "Universities of" have. So, as a lover of underdogs, I always root for the state colleges.

And, I'm happy to say, things have never been better for the downtrodden State U's. Colorado State whipped the University of Colorado again. Both Iowa State and Oklahoma State finally beat the University of Nebraska. Isn't that one fine how-do-you-do? Washington State and North Carolina State are the world-beaters in their states. Okay, Florida State has had a down season, but it has been a national champion twice in recent years. Kansas State used to be the absolute worst team in the country, but now it's a perennial top-twenty-five team. Virginia Tech, which is actually Virginia Polytechnic and State U., is leaving Mr. Jefferson's stately University of Virginia in its dust. Utah State has finally found a conference that will take it in. Why, the state of the State U teams hasn't been so fine since that glorious day when Larry Bird left Indiana University for Indiana State and then led his team into the NCAA championship game against Michigan State.

The *only* State U's I don't root for are Ohio State, Louisiana State, and Penn State, because even though they are State U's, they have always been the real top teams in their state. They have no business being State U's. As for Arizona and Arizona State, I can't tell them apart.

State U's don't have nearly as much tradition as universities-of. They don't have the good rivalries. They don't have the beloved indigenous nicknames like the Terps or the Razorbacks or the Fightin' Illini or the Hoosiers or the Jayhawks. Instead, State U's are left with generic hand-me-down nicknames like the Redbirds or the Wolfpack or the Hornets or the Wildcats.

State U's don't have any upscale addresses either. Athletes who play for teams at universities-of always identify themselves with the name of their school town. It sounds so much more elegant, so private school. I go to Madison. I go to Boulder. I go to Chapel Hill. I go to Berkeley. State U players just go to state. Very few people even know where State U's are.

So here's to the upwardly mobile teams, the downscale strivers. To all the State U's, and to the techs and A&Ms . . . and most of all, may I cheer loudest for the teams that don't even have a whole state. Go, Southern Mississippi. Hooray for Northern Illinois. I'm with you, Southeast Missouri. Kick butt, Middle Tennessee. They're all living the American Dream, athletic division.

The Fenway Park Address

2004

As Abraham Lincoln spoke to Red Sox fans the other day:

"Fourscore and six years ago, our fathers saw before them, in this city, in Fenway Park, a world's championship, granted Boston by the Red Sox, and dedicated to the proposition that as there had been so many before, so would so many more so soon follow.

"Now we are engaged again in a great series, testing whether, without victory, this city or any city so dedicated to the national pastime can long endure. For it is our sorrow that we, the heirs of Pilgrims past, have not enjoyed so much as one diamond diadem ever since. We are met again on two great ball fields—the one down within the Bronx, where a pinstriped plethora of world championship banners wave with every gentle zephyr; the other here in the hallowed Fens, where, instead, it is but two monsters that loom above us—the one a wall so green as it is high and wide, the other a thing larger yet in our misery, a spectral curse that covers us as a shroud. It is altogether fitting and proper that we should rid ourselves of this greater monster.

"But, in a larger sense, we cannot overcome—we cannot triumph—we cannot conquer—this October—any October— until we forgive all those brave BoSox who lost their noble reputations in certain cursed Series past. This world will little note nor long remember that we won the wild card or mopped up the Anaheim Angels until we, the loyal fans of this century, yet descended from the Royal Rooters of yore, grant to goats past our full pardon for the expiation of their calamitous transgressions. Especially, it falls to us, the living spectators, to forever forget the deadly sins past, put out from our minds that the poor Pesky held the ball, that the woeful Buckner could not grasp the ball, nor that the misguided Little would not take the ball from Pedro. Those honored Sox have given the last measure of their reputation so that we citizens might actually revel in our melancholy, even as we pretend to despise our despair.

"Now we must resolve to exculpate all who have, in their wayward exercise, cost us victories we believe were our rightful due. Above all, if we are at last to whip the Evil Empire and raise the championship ensign where for so long a curse has lain upon us, we of the Red Sox nation, under God, must banish all thoughts of that one grandest hero, once ours, so that memories of the Babe, by the Bambino, for the Sultan of Swat, shall yet perish from the Hub."

Getting to
Know You

2002

Every time an NFL or college football factory hires a new coach these days, the race of the man is called to attention. Two sports that African Americans dominate post quite different records in the coaching ranks, though. In basketball, almost half of the pro coaches are black, and so are almost a quarter of Division-I college coaches.

But only three NFL teams had black coaches this past season, and that's down to two now, while among the colleges the only big-time African American coach is Tyrone Willingham, who's moved up from Stanford to Notre Dame. There are a number of reasons to account for this, beginning with the root differences between the games themselves. Basketball is a pretty intimate enterprise, with only a handful of players on a team. Even the substitutes can emerge as personalities. And remember, it's the benchwarmers in all sports who usually make the best coaches. The incumbent coaches, owners, athletic directors, and general managers get to know their basketball players well. They're distinct people, not just guys in helmets, which is what so many football players are.

Besides, coaching basketball depends so much on the personal element. A football coach can be a distant workaholic, organizing, organizing. A basketball coach, though, can't last unless his players certify him as a human being. He has assistants, but the system is not so hierarchical. Secure NBA coaches now often even keep wise old strategists around to advise them. These septuagenarian ex–head coaches are sort of like consultants, the medicine men of team sports. Basketball is more familial, more tribal; football more structured, more corporate. Football coaches are executives. They have vice presidents, offensive and defensive coordinators, and middle management department heads in charge of the myriad positions.

So not only do the people who hire football coaches probably fail to get to know young black coaching candidates; there is surely some kind of submerged racism which presumes: "Sure, a black man can handle a little basketball club, but a heavy-duty football operation is really too complicated to trust to a minority." Athletic directors have also been known to whisper that wealthy alumni wouldn't stand for a black coach. It's the same secret excuse they used years ago, saying alumni wouldn't tolerate black players.

General managers and athletic directors likewise protest too much, but they won't hire a black coach because they'll get too much heat when they eventually fire him. I first heard this thirty years ago in basketball. I asked a potential black coach what he thought of that. He only turned, and smiling, quoted Tennyson to me: "'Tis better to have loved and lost than never to have loved at all."

Patriot Games

1996

At the time when Samuel Johnson observed, "Patriotism is the last refuge of a scoundrel," big-time international sports was not yet conceived. Today, it's fair to say that "patriotism is the last, best gimmick of a sports promoter."

The idea that it is an *obligation* for top athletes to play games on behalf of their fellow countrymen—that is one of the great emotional cons. The unctuous phrase always used to coerce athletes into helping some promoter make a buck in the name of national interest is that "it is an honor to represent your country." This, predictably, is what Juan Antonio Samaranch, the pretentious impresario of the Olympics, parroted, when I asked him why Olympic athletes shouldn't be paid wages for providing the entertainment that makes all sorts of money for all sorts of other people. *Oh, but it is an honor to represent your country.*

But for some reason it doesn't seem to be honor enough for promoters and television announcers and marketing executives and agents and all the other sharpies who make money off international sport to help represent their country for free. They are honored with cash. If it's sauce for the goose, why isn't it sauce for the leech? If athletes are expected to represent their country for free, fine—but then so should everybody else give up any remuneration.

The issue has at last been forced onto the table in golf, where some of the top American golfers—notably Tiger Woods, Mark O'Meara, and David Duval—have questioned why they should be required to accept a measly $5,000 stipend for playing in the Ryder Cup, an event now worth $63 million. Naturally, they've been called selfish ingrates. Ben Crenshaw, the captain of the American team, has made the point that Woods, O'Meara, and Duval are denigrating the memory of "those who came before them."

Crenshaw is a very sincere person, and he is also one of those who did come before. But times—and economics—have changed. Crenshaw, for example, conspicuously wears a hat advertising Buick, whenever he plays. And the Ryder Cup used to be a pleasant anachronism played between the Brits and the Yanks before a few friends and family. Now it's a Euro-American television extravaganza. Likewise, once upon a time, the Olympics were amateur championships contested by some weekend hobbyists. Now the Olympics produce billions in revenue, and competitors must devote their whole lives to training. The idea that they should donate their services, in the interest of national amusement, so that others might get rich, is one of the grandest hypocrisies extant.

Anyway, the whole fiction that golfers and swimmers and ice skaters and soccer players "represent" their country is so much balderdash. Madeleine Albright represents this country. Richard Holbrook represents this country. And, by the by, they get paid for it. Simply putting on a uniform that says "USA," instead of "Celtics" or "Red Wings" or "Buick," doesn't invest an athlete with any national property.

Yes, in that awful, smarmy phrase, many athletes do indeed "give back to the game." But nobody has a right to force talented men and women to provide pro bono patriotism—especially no rich guy in a blazer, sitting in a corporate tent, stuffing in free crab cakes and martinis, who has never once himself sacrificed any of his time or treasure for the honor of representing his country.

August Song

2009

Of all the months of the year, during all my years, the month that's changed the most is August.

Don't you think so? Once upon a time, August was just sort of a valuable nowhere time that got us safely, leisurely from the peak heat of July to the autumn of September, when everything would begin again.

Nothing much happened in August. There are no songs about August, no August-April romances. It's one of the few months without any sort of holiday.

The president invariably would vacation in August, and Congress would close up shop, and we'd be blissfully newsless. There were only reruns on television, so you didn't have to watch anything.

If life was a game, August was a time-out.

The only major August sports event is the PGA golf tournament, which was held last week in Minnesota. August was always the perfect time for the PGA, which is sort of a redundant Grand Slam, a Class-B U.S. Open.

So August was a nice respite. We needed August. Then things changed. First, everybody started going back to school before Labor Day. Who'd ever heard of such a thing?

Then everybody started saying "24-7." That put the pressure on August to stop being so lazy and catch up with all the other twenty-fours and sevens. August just wasn't pulling its load. So they started television series in August. *Mad Men* has already begun again. Now you have to pay attention and remember what's happened.

Not only that, but high schools and colleges started playing football in August.

Baseball is better suited for August. It's not so energetic and full bore. Besides, not only is football so downright aggressive, but there's a seasonal symbolism to football. Football means business.

People always rhapsodize about how the beginning of baseball best symbolizes the spring of life, la-di-da. But football has more substantive symbolism. Spring comes at different times in different parts of America, but buckling down after the summer comes all at once, all over.

Now the NFL, watching August being carved up like Yugoslavia, is contemplating getting its share, too—increasing its schedule from sixteen games to eighteen. That'll be the final straw: when the NFL storms into August. Then the August we knew and needed will be gone forever. August will just be a suburb of September, and, gee, I think we'll all be the poorer for it.

The Rev. Mr. Coach

2002

Even before the pedophilia scandal erupted in the Roman Catholic Church, unsettling reports of athletic coaches molesting their players had begun to bubble up. Most prominently, an NHL player finally found the nerve to speak out against a coach who had abused him years before in a youth hockey league. And Pete Sampras's first coach was sent to jail for molesting his tennis students, even if Sampras himself had never been a victim.

But on a wider level, all sorts of coaches of young boys in many sports have been found guilty of predatory sexual charges, some against many of their players over the span of many years. Just last week in New York, the kindly benefactor of a legendary teenage boys' basketball church program was accused of molestation. Horrible as it is to contemplate priests, men of God, taking advantage of young boys, it's perhaps an even greater violation of trust for coaches to be predators. A priest, after all, is but a surrogate of God; a coach often appears to a young boy as the Almighty himself here on Earth.

There is, for example, the old joke about Jesus and a powerful coach walking along together. Someone says, "Isn't that God?" And his friend says, "No, that's Coach Jones. He only thinks he's God."

More to the earthly point, coaches determine the immediate fate of boys more than do clergy. Coaches, after all, determine if you make the team, how much you play. Most boys are far more in the thrall of a man with a whistle than of one with a crucifix. Indeed, coaches play such a significant role in the life of children that it's not uncommon for a grown athlete to look back and say that such and such a coach was by far the most important adult in his life, or, anyway, second only to his father. Coaches on the field enjoy a close position of trust, even of love, that few teachers in the classroom ever attain.

It is not either just the coaches of boys who sometimes abuse this honorable status. There have been scandals involving female coaches having lesbian love affairs or seeking same with their college players. And the salacious reports of middle-aged male tennis coaches seducing their teenage female protégées as they conveniently toured the world together became so prominent that the Women's Tennis Association, which once turned its head away from the obvious, has now wisely instituted careful monitoring.

To be sure, most coaches, like most priests, are not sexual predators. In sports, the most famous pedophile was, in fact, a star player, the tennis world champion Big Bill Tilden, an emotionally and sexually stunted adult who usually traveled with a boy companion. Twice Tilden would be jailed for sexual misconduct with adolescents. But also we cannot be naive. Pedophiles are obviously going to be attracted to coaching boys. It's an all-male situation rife with physicality, where the coach has power, mystique, and accessibility.

Sport is religion to many people, especially to many boys who could be so susceptible to men they admire and effectively worship, men they devotedly call "coach."

An update:
Like so many commentaries that I had forgotten about until I started going over them to make selections for this book, I had forgotten this one. It makes it all the more difficult to believe that so many people, Joe Paterno included, could profess to be so without guile when, years later, Jerry Sandusky's true self was revealed. Obviously, there have always been more pedophiles in coaching than we have wanted to believe.

Used to Be

2014

When I was a young, cocksure lad in this business, one thing I hated was for anyone in the Old Guard to preface an observation about sports by saying, "It used to be . . ." Invariably, the point was that it used to be better. I promised myself that I'd never become a "used-to-be" guy. But for the benefit of today's young, cocksure lads in the business, here I go:

- It used to be that people always asked me if these athletes weren't making too much money. Nobody ever asks me that anymore. The only money issue I hear now is, "Why aren't college athletes paid?"

- It used to be that people always complained to me about how television was taking over sports, with TV time-outs and different starting times. Nobody ever complains about that to me anymore. Ever. All they complain about now is when they can't get a game they want to see on TV.

- It used to be that people asked me how many games were really fixed, because they'd heard it was lots. As if I knew. Instead people ask me how many athletes are doping, because they heard, for sure, that it's lots more.

- It used to be that people would ask me why Americans didn't like soccer. Now people ask me why the American media won't give soccer its proper due because Americans really, really do like soccer.

- It used to be that people wanted to know if athletes actually cheated on their wives so much on the road. Nobody ever asks me that anymore. Instead, they ask me if I think sports contribute to misogyny, because so many athletes are involved in brutal sexual assaults on women.

- It used to be that people always asked me who I thought the greatest boxer was, as if I knew. They stopped asking that, and then it used to be they'd ask me if boxing was ever going to come back. Nobody ever asks me anything about boxing anymore. Anything. Ever.

- It used to be that people would tell me all the time how sports build character. Now that athletes are regularly arrested for violent crimes, and so many college athletes are participating in a giant fraud that the academic community supports, people don't tell me this anymore. Instead, they ask me, dubiously, "Do you really think sports build character?"

- It used to be that people would tell me they were going out to play golf. I don't hear that much anymore, except from old folks. Now people tell me they can't play golf because they have to work longer hours and it takes too long.

- It used to be that people would always ask me who I thought was going to win the game. As if I knew. Now people always ask me who I think is going to win the game. As if I know. Well, some things never change.

FOURTEEN

Blessed Are the Pure

2012

Certain forms of art are performed in private. The painter is alone when he paints, the writer likewise.

But the most pertinent aspect of the performing arts is that they are watched. Dance, music, drama, and sport are most challenging—and most thrilling—precisely because they are real, before our eyes.

All of them, of course, can be tainted by human foibles. We make athletes heroes at our peril. Athletes, for example, fix games. They cheat when they can. They can be cruel on the field, and off it violent brutes—especially in their treatment of women. Just read the paper any day and be disappointed.

But all of these iniquities taken together do not violate sport as much as drugs do alone. Athletics, like the other performing arts, is primarily a function of the body. Yes, it helps to understand well the game you are playing, but, ultimately, sports are physical. They require strength, speed, balance, hand-eye coordination, and, often, endurance. To succeed, the athlete must excel in at least one of these qualities or even, in some cases, in a mixture of all. At base, we attend games and we become sports fans because we are enthralled that these young men and women are capable, with their bodies, of what we could never manage with ours. We envy and cheer their graceful superiority.

When athletes take performance-enhancing drugs they destroy that basic truth. Imagine if there were a drug that could improve a tenor's or a soprano's voice, so the notes were purer. That would devalue all opera because the art would be false; the cognoscenti would be unable to trust what they heard as true human beauty.

Think of that analogy with steroids and HGH in sport.

Visual entertainment certainly doesn't need to be real. Magicians have always performed what they frankly call "tricks." The movies now live by what are advertised as "special effects." But in sports, the bodies must be honest or what's the point? In a horrible way, concussions are good for football; they validate how seriously the bodies function in that game. You need a few matadors gored to sell bullfight tickets.

But drugs—Lance Armstrong on the highest level, and lesser lights like Melky Cabrera and Bartolo Colon—don't just poison the game. They poison our faith. It's only natural now that every rational person must at least wonder whenever any athlete, no matter how revered, does something exceptional. We've been surprised too often, disillusioned too often, suckered too often, hurt too often.

So eventually, we might doubt all the bodies. And if you doubt the voices, there is no opera; if you doubt the bodies, there is no sport. It becomes just another entertainment with special effects.

That's why drugs are more of a threat to sport than all the other abuses and deceits put together.

Speaking of Sports

1999

I am informed by the *American Journalism Review* that a survey of almost three hundred broadcast students at three major journalism schools reveals that better than half the males want to go into sports. In particular, among the young American men who aspire to actually be on the air, more than twice as many would rather cover games instead of news.

I suppose I should be delighted at this revelation. After all, as someone who's been a sports journalist for most of my working life, these figures would be affirming of my vocation. But still, proud though I may be of my profession, it never occurred to me that it was meant to be a working *majority*. That more than half of young men in TV would want to cover sports has the same ring to it as if we learned that more than half the males in medical school wanted to concentrate on cosmetic surgery.

The contrary news, by the way, is that only 8 percent of the aspiring *female* broadcasters want to go into sports—which also means, by process of elimination, that soon most all the anchors and reporters on television will be women.

More important, this is just another example of the sportification of our society. It indicates how so many more young people—well, young males—are determined to go into sports, even if they can't *play* sports. For instance, one of the most popular new majors on campus is sports management, wherein you study to become a general manager. Oh my, the nerds are invading sports, too.

But then, it's difficult not to also conclude that as women infiltrate positions of authority in almost all professions, at least a certain number of insecure men will turn to sports business as the last mostly male power refuge.

Yet more evidence is that more and more old, terribly rich men seek to cap their careers by buying sports teams. It's the best way to let everybody know you're really rich, owning a team.

Still, it never fails to amaze moral custodians that most taxpayers are delighted to pay for stadiums and arenas and donate all sorts of additional goodies to the fabulously wealthy men who own the teams. Rationally, of course, it makes no sense that the poorer people in our society will pay for stadiums that benefit the richest, and newspaper editorialists are always hysterically emphasizing how foolish the people are.

But, of course, the citizens continue to vote that way because that's how the system works—if you wants sports in your city. It's very much a medieval arrangement. Back then, the serfs contributed crops to the lord of the castle, because he provided protection. Today, the taxpayers contribute to the lord of the stadium because he provides amusement.

Likewise, why would any American boy want to grow up, to stand at risk in some dangerous war zone, shouting news into a microphone, when he could be seated comfortably behind home plate or above the eighteenth green, safe and peaceful, telling the guys all about what really concerns them—the fun and games?

An update:
Well, let's see what's changed since I wrote this at the end of last century.

- *I don't know how many male broadcast students still want to go into sports, but clearly more females do. Whereas, at least in men's sports, virtually all the play-by-play announcers and analysts (old jocks) are still men, a majority of the sideline reporters are women. There are also female sports anchors now. Women are simply pretty common in television sports journalism now. Helps to be pretty, of course.*
- *Many of the 92 percent of aspiring female broadcasters not interested in covering sports have hit their mark. I'm constantly amazed at how many women are now war correspondents.*
- *In the matter of owning teams, though, that's still the province of rich old men. Rich old women haven't gotten around to that yet. But clearly that will come to pass when today's rich middle-aged women get a little older.*

Life Among the Idle Fans

2006

Do you get the feeling that there are really no more stadiums and arenas being built in the United States? All these palaces where sports are played are flying up all over. But what they really seem to be are just a bunch of luxury boxes that happen to be attached to a few hard grandstand seats. The profit in sports comes from selling luxury boxes to expense accounts in swells.

So, take me up to the luxury box, take me off from the crowd.

Give me some champagne and caviar. I don't care if they even keep score.

Let me call, call, call for the waitress.

If she won't come it's a pox.

For it's one, two, three kinds of wine at the old luxury box.

And boy, have you peasants ever been in one? Boy, are luxury boxes wonderful.

The booze, the fine food, the service, the private powder rooms. Best of all, especially at a freezing-cold football game, is deigning to glance down upon sad hoi polloi just outside your luxury box, their lips blue, their bodies shivering as they look back at you with wistful, longing eyes like poor urchins at the window of the pastry shop. It's glorious.

Being in a luxury box is better even than not having to pay any estate tax. Isn't it paradoxical, too? Sports are supposed to be for the masses, yet you will not find luxury boxes at the opera or the ballet. Even when you get a house seat on Broadway, that's all you get, a seat: just the place to rest your backside. Only in sports do we generally find plush, sumptuous, lavish condominium accommodations.

So can you believe it? There is actually a place in America today where humble citizens are fighting the construction of luxury boxes. Yes, in Ann Arbor, Michigan, home of what is called the Big House—the largest stadium in America—many alumni and professors of the University of Michigan are vigorously trying to convince the Board of Regents not to approve the plans of the university president and the athletic director to spend something like a quarter of a billion dollars to build seventy-eight suites that would rent at up to $85,000 apiece for a mere seven college football games.

The Big House is a huge oval and the luxury boxes, totaling 425,000 square feet, would do great aesthetic violence to the classical bowl. Since the game day pieds-à-terre would cost so much to build, it's even dubious that they can actually make the university any money. That, after all, is the whole purpose of luxury boxes.

So finally, somewhere in the republic, the lowly common folk have risen up against the sports aristocracy. So let us with them give new voice to that big Michigan fight song, "Hail to the Victors."

Hail to the fat cats dining.
Hail to the privileged gentry.
Hail, hail to luxury box, the poshest and the best.
Hail to the nouveau drinking.
Hail to the high-hat blue bloods.
Hail, hail to luxury box, the measure of success.

The regents' vote is set for Friday.

Juiced

2000

This much we know. More players hit more home runs than ever before. But we don't know why. Why do you think? Go on, say it. I'll wait. . . . I know what you just said: "Well, *they've* juiced up the ball."

Everybody says this. Everybody has been saying this forever. It is the most popular conspiracy theory in sport. In fact, even the smartest experts blithely say it. *Sports Illustrated* just tossed it off last week in its lead editorial: "juiced balls." Pick up a newspaper, turn on the radio or TV: "they're juicing up the ball."

May I once again ask a question: *who* is juicing the balls up? And another question: *how* are *they* doing it? Even the idiotic conspiracy theories about the grassy knoll or Vince Foster's suicide include purported details of how it really was supposed to happen. But for all those people who are so convinced that *they* juice up the balls, nobody ever tries to explain how *they* would go about this.

I spoke to Sandy Alderson, the commissioner's right-hand man. (I couldn't ask the commissioner himself, because a lot of the conspiracy nuts figure he's the culprit.) Could *they* be the owners? I asked Sandy. We laughed at the very thought that thirty baseball owners could assemble and conspire and then all thirty could take the secret to their grave.

Well, could it be the commissioner? Alderson pointed out that, in fact, until this year, the commissioner didn't even have anything to do with the balls. It was in the domain of the league presidents, who would've had to plot together. These guys couldn't even agree on the designated hitter. They were going to *conspire* to doctor balls made in Costa Rica?

Alderson pointed out that since one ball is tested from each lot, if the commissioner, Bud Selig, was, all by himself, scheming to juice up the balls, he would have to go secretly to Costa Rica, and then, not only order the formula changed, but also demand that one ball in each lot be made to the old specifications so that it could pass tests. That's a powerful lot of conspiracy.

"Maybe the '*they*' is a wildcatter," Alderson suggested, helpfully. "Somebody mysterious who works for Rawlings"—the company that makes the balls—"is doing this on a lark."

"Or," I replied, "a Svengali who, every morning, hypnotizes the women who make the balls in Costa Rica."

Well, conspiracy fans, I'm sorry, but those are your only choices.

Baseballs are not juiced up—simply because it is impossible for anybody to do it alone, just as it is impossible for a *bunch* of people to conspire to do it and keep it a secret.

Rather, here are the probable reasons that players hit more home runs nowadays:

The parks are smaller and customized to reward power.

Striking out is not the stigma it used to be, so all players whale away, trying to hit more home runs.

Lighting is better than ever, and, as Alderson points out, vision is so correctable now that everybody can see the ball better.

Umpires have, through the years, shrunk the strike zone to the batters' advantage.

And, surely most important, like other modern athletes, hitters are bigger and stronger than ever. So, of course, are the pitchers, but whereas power hitting is primarily a function of strength, pitching is a learned craft. And there are simply not that many good pitchers who have learned how to pitch well.

If you want to believe that *they* are secretly juicing up the ball, may I suggest you move to Roswell, New Mexico, and chat with our high government officials who are sleeping there with beautiful little green aliens.

An update:

How dumb could I be? All the reasons I suggested for why more home runs were being hit, and it didn't even occur to me that the real reason was steroids.

I take some comfort from the fact that I had a lot of ignorant company.

Of course, it is interesting that now that the worm has turned and pitchers are dominating, you never hear a word spoken about juiced balls—which, I think, helps prove my point that the balls are not juiced. Just the players.

And just as it was suggested then that the umpires must have shrunk the strike zone, now that pitching rules it is bruited that umpires have expanded the strike zone. Probably the same strike zone.

Don't Tie One On

2012

Politicians love to boast about American exceptionalism: how special we are from all the merely ordinary, everyday, run-of-the-mill countries around the globe. I would say that what sets us apart, more all the time, is that we Americans don't like ties. I don't mean four-in-hands or bow ties, but the ties in games, the ones that somebody once said are "like kissing your sister."

Boy, do I agree. Nothing about me is more American than the fact that I don't like ties. Lots of times, in other English-speaking countries, a tie is called a draw. Well, partner, in these United States, when we say "draw," we don't mean a namby-pamby even Stephen—we mean John Wayne a-reachin' for his six-shooter. Now that's the American way to draw, a-standin' our ground.

Okay, we used to countenance tie games. Look back through the records, and you'll see that in the olden days, all football teams played lots of ties. For the best teams, the expression even went, "unbeaten and untied."

Nobody says that anymore. You're either beat, or doing the beating—no Mr. In-Between. College football changed the rules in 1996, so two teams keep playing until somebody wins. The NFL is still a little wimpish. There have been two NFL ties in the twenty-first century—two too many, in the minds of good red-blooded Americans like me.

Ice hockey was tie city. I blame that on the Canadians, who are so nice. But now, in hockey, we got shootouts. That's the all-American way. There hasn't been a tie in the NHL since April 4, 2004. And there never will be another.

The worst thing that happened to baseball since steroids was when they ran out of pitchers at the 2002 All-Star Game, and it was called a draw. A date that will live on in stupidity. Do you know they have ties in Japanese baseball? That just flat-out takes the "national" out of "pastime."

But of course, the rest of the world loves soccer. And it is reliably calculated that 30 percent of all soccer games end tied, drawn, deadlocked, nil-nil. How does the rest of the unexceptional world tolerate this? It's exactly this kind of thinking, I believe, which is why they can't fix the bloody euro. The dollar is a winner. The euro is a tie. Get off the dime, Europe, and play to win.

In this country, the teams in Major League Soccer play a thirty-four-game schedule. They averaged eleven ties a team. Chicago had sixteen ties out of thirty-four! Couldn't they at least get rid of ties in American soccer?

A tie has no place in sports. It's like not finding out who is the "who" in a whodunit.

Paying Through the Noseguard

2011

Hollywood inhabitants always joke that nobody can understand the profit and loss statements of films. There's an old expression: "We shoulda shot the deal instead of the movie—it's got a better plot." The same, it seems to me, could be said of the economics of college athletics.

Now college football—it's incredibly popular: filling stadiums, pulling down lollapalooza television money, selling oodles of high-priced memorabilia. Plus, on top of all that, the performers—the players—don't get paid a penny. Not even Hollywood producers can work that scam. But still, only fourteen athletic departments show a profit.

That's because football—perhaps with some help from men's basketball—must pick up the bills for all the many other sports that lose money.

However, it's often the case that the charity sports still operate on the luxurious revenue sport model. In a fascinating article on Bloomberg.com about athletics at Rutgers, the State University of New Jersey, authors Curtis Eichelberger and Oliver Staley point out that the Scarlet Knights' women's basketball coach made $1.3 million a year, plus allowances for a car and golf—yes, golf—even though last year the program drew barely three thousand fans to home games and lost $2.2 million.

Meanwhile, forty professors in the history department at Rutgers had their telephones removed due to budget cuts.

The Big East added that well-known East Coast team, Texas Christian, as a football member. That's nothing. The small-time Eastern Collegiate Athletic Association now has teams located from Connecticut to Colorado. In lacrosse.

Look, I'm all for the wonderful intrinsic values of sport: exercise and competition and team spirit—but especially in these parlous economic times, couldn't many minor college sports be conducted on an intramural basis? Would the universities' educational missions be diminished by that decision? Would good student applicants reject them for lack of league lacrosse games? Come on.

Clark Kerr, who was the head of the California university system back when "California education" was not an oxymoron, opined that the modern American university's purpose "has come to be defined as providing parking for the faculty, sex for the students, and athletics for the alumni." Okay, given that student sex and faculty parking are a given, couldn't we just switch most intercollegiate athletics to the intramural? Surely, there are enough professional teams for the alumni to turn to for their amusement.

All the worse, the current national model has it that some impoverished kid from the inner city risks concussions and obesity to play football in order to pay for the scholarship of a javelin thrower and the salary of an assistant swimming coach and the plane fare for the volleyball team. That's a disgrace. Where is it written that that's the way an athletic department should be operated, on the shoulder pads of poor kids and the telephonic deprivations of poor history professors?

"Instead of dirt and poison, we have rather chosen to fill our hives with honey and wax, thus furnishing mankind with the two noblest of things, which are sweetness and light."

—Jonathan Swift

Sweetness and Light

2012

At Christmastime, it's long been the fashion for sports columnists to write an annual column about what various people in sports want to find under their trees—a new quarterback for this coach, a starting pitcher for this general manager, and so on.

But, of course, the Christmas of Santa Claus isn't the only one. There's also the message that is found in the Gospel of Luke, which we can all of us, of all faiths, support—as the angels sing: And on earth, peace, goodwill among people.

Nothing is so down-to-earth as sports, so let us, this morning, take scripture rather than Santa, and celebrate just some of the peace and goodwill we'd like to find in sport in the year ahead:

First, of all, most obviously, may the National Hockey League owners and players find labor peace and start the season.

May all men and women who coach children's teams treat their young charges with kindness. Character does not have to be built with screaming and abuse. May children's sports coaches show the same goodwill as those who direct children in plays and conduct them in orchestras.

And may all parents, watching their children play youth games, act with grace toward their own kids and goodwill toward all the others.

May Manny Pacquiao have the good sense never to climb back into the ring again. You were the best, Manny, but now go away in peace, and don't risk the good life you can lead for yourself and your Philippine people.

Hey: At every stadium and every arena, when you hear "Down in front," get down.

Find a way to persuade National Football League players to stop owning guns and carrying guns. Peace, guys.

Have European soccer fans stop being racist. Goodwill, chaps and amigos.

May Pat Summitt, the great Tennessee coach, find joy in the games she still can watch and a gentle comfort thereafter.

Whenever the NHL does come back, let's make hockey like every other civilized sport and ban fighting.

May all networks give us more peace and quiet by restricting the call to two announcers per game, per booth.

For every fan at every game who has ever had a beer: if you have to get drunk when rooting for your team, have the courtesy to stay home and watch the game there on your big HD screen in the family room.

May every football player—NFL, college, high school, Pop Warner—have the good sense to tackle with your shoulder, rather than spear with your head. Peace, goodwill to all players.

And, when you go to the game, whatever the game, watch your language and turn off your cell phone. Peace. Goodwill to all fans.